Getting to Know the New Testament

Stephen H. Travis

CLEMENTS PUBLISHING
Toronto, Ontario

Getting to Know the New Testament

This edition published 2004 by
Clements Publishing
213-6021 Yonge Street
Toronto, Ontario
M2M 3W2 Canada
www.clementspublishing com

National Library of Canada Cataloguing in Publication Data

Travis, Stephen H

Getting to know the New Testament / Stephen H Travis

ISBN 1-894667-34-4

1 Bible. N T.—Criticism, interpretation, etc. I Title.

BS2361 3.T73 2003 225.6'1 C2003-90363

Contents

Foreword

'Do you understand what you are reading?', said Philip the evangelist to the Ethiopian treasury official, as he struggled through his scroll of Isaiah (Acts 8.30). It's a question to which all of us from time to time answer, 'Not really'. Yet many people today are discovering in the Bible the message which brings them closer to Christ, the giver of life in all its fullness. Some study it regularly on their own, others meet in groups to share their insights and their questions. As I've been writing this book, I've tried to imagine people getting involved in such groups, perhaps for the first time in their lives. And I've tried to set out in the book what I would want to share with them if they were generous enough to give me nine or ten weekly sessions to explain how the New Testament may be approached.

There are difficulties in understanding most kinds of book, until you get the hang of it. And there are particular difficulties with an ancient book such as the New Testament. There are some books on understanding the Bible which seem to tell you fifteen things you must get right before you can hope to read the Bible properly. That's enough to switch some of us off for ever. So I've tried a different approach.

I'm writing this in a break between matches at Wimbledon. As I've watched these geniuses at play, I've been asking myself, 'How did they learn?' One thing's certain. They didn't learn by reading books which told them fifteen things they must get right before they walk on court. They learnt by playing. They probably played badly at first, but with practice and guidance they improved. So now they know all about sliced services and top-spin lobs and double-handed backhands down the line. These things have been gradually built into their game till they could do them in their sleep.

Well, people who are ready for complicated books about the finer techniques of New Testament interpretation can find them elsewhere. My book is for people who are not sure they can even get the ball over the net. But they want to improve their game. So I've kept it as straightforward as I reasonably can, and I've included plenty of examples – demonstrations of the main strokes which we need to master if we are to improve our game. At the end of each chapter is a summary of its contents and a set of suggestions for group study (which could also be used for personal reflection). At the end of the book there are suggestions about basic helps to bible study. All biblical quotations are from the *Good News Bible*, and I recommend that readers have a copy of this translation handy.

Like any author, I am in debt to many people, including those who have written more complicated books on the New Testament and its meaning. Also, Nigel Stone has provided the example of different understandings of time in chapter one; Robert Barlow and Junction 25, the drama group of St John's College, Nottingham, are responsible for the sketch in chapter three; Carol Bebawi has turned my pencilled scrawl into clear typescript, and my family have been extremely good-humoured as I worked odd hours to get the book finished. To them all I offer my warm thanks.

1

The New Testament – strange yet powerful

The New Testament is an exciting book. It turns people's lives upside-down. Leaping over barriers of time, language and culture, it wriggles into people's consciousness and transforms them.

A prisoner in England had been written off as a hopeless case by psychiatrists and prison officers. Desperately worried about his wife, who was heading for a serious illness, he did what prisoners often do. Having run out of paper to roll a cigarette, he tore a page out of the *Gideon Bible* which lay in his cell. Words from John's Gospel, chapter fourteen, leapt out at him: 'If you ask anything in my name, I will do it'. He didn't know how to pray. He had never learnt the Lord's Prayer. His only religious upbringing was three or four visits to the Band of Hope before being expelled for misbehaviour. But he found himself falling to his knees, confessing his sins, asking God to make a new man of him and to care for his wife. He discovered a God ready to forgive and to change him. Through an experience of the living God, which began from a single verse of scripture, a 'hopeless case' became a man who would bring hope to others.

A Russian teenager living in Paris around 1930, was aggressively anti-christian and hated everything to do with God. After listening unwillingly to a talk by a priest, he decided to read a gospel to check whether the priest's picture of Christianity – which the young man found repulsive – was supported by the gospel account. Not to waste time unnecessarily, he chose Mark, the shortest gospel. Before he reached the third chapter, he suddenly became aware that on the other side of his desk stood the risen Jesus. His hostility crumbled away and he became a disciple of Christ. Today he is Metropolitan Anthony, the Russian Orthodox Archbishop in London.

In Malawi a village evangelist told the story of Zacchaeus, from Luke 19, to a group of men gathered for worship of their ancestors. They believed that their dead ancestors controlled the lives of the living and were responsible for rain and harvests. The evangelist's teaching led several men to accept Christ, and since then many others have become believers. The coming of Christianity to the village has meant not only the burning of objects used in witchcraft and of shrines for ancestor worship, but also the restoring of marriages and reduction of various kinds of evil. Young people are eager to study the scriptures. The evangelist says, 'Without the Bible we are nowhere'. A whole community has been transformed.

Thousands of such stories could be reported from every continent. For most of us, the New Testament's influence is less dramatic. Yet we too can speak of how its message has brought us to God, fed our prayers, nudged us into action. And this book is about how we can get the message out of the New Testament, understand it, and let it get to work on us.

Yet, although christians find that the Bible speaks to them in a way which is true of no other book, understanding it is not a straightforward matter. Sometimes, as we have seen, God reveals himself through its words with a power which shakes, and rebuilds, the foundations of people's lives, but often passages in the New Testament are puzzling, obscure. Their meaning can be misunderstood, or twisted to fit in with the interpreter's own ideas. There was a fifteenth century sect in Bohemia, called the Adamites, which taught that marriage between one husband and one wife was a sin, since the Bible commands us to have all things in common. They practised free love, and on the strength of Jesus' announcement that 'tax collectors and prostitutes are going into the Kingdom of God ahead of you' (Matthew 21.31), they declared that the chaste were unworthy to join their community!

Not many people distort the New Testament's meaning as violently as that. But we often find it hard to understand, or easy to misunderstand. Why should this be? After all, most of us who pick up a newspaper or a paperback novel at a station bookstall haven't taken lessons in 'Understanding Newspapers', or 'How to Interpret a Novel'. So why is the Bible a problem? The difficulty arises because the Bible is an old book; and we have to come to terms with that.

The strangeness of the New Testament

'The past is a foreign country: they do things differently there.' This first sentence of L. P. Hartley's novel, *The Go-Between*, sums up our problem. Our world is very different from the world of two hundred years ago, let alone two thousand years. Most obviously, society and its customs have changed. Most of us live in cities: we do not experience or understand the rhythms and customs of village life which figure so centrally in the teaching of Jesus. If there are children in our cities who don't realize that milk comes from cows, what chance have we of appreciating the finer points of parables about shepherds, sowers and vine-growers? And the society to which Jesus and his first followers belonged was a society which took for granted the subjection of women, the existence of slavery, and other customs which are strange or abhorrent to us.

Another thing which has changed is the way people view the past. Until about the eighteenth century, people looked to the past for wisdom and authority. They turned to ancient Greek philosophers, and of course to Moses and Jesus, for answers to their questions about life. Old people were respected for their wisdom and experience. But today most people don't expect to find answers in the past. Technology and psychiatry will solve our problems, we imagine.

The most important change has come about, however, not in the nature of society and its customs, nor in our attitude to the past, but in the way we understand the world. The growth of science and thought in the last three hundred years has seen to that. In the first century it was generally believed that the world was flat, with heaven – and God – above, and the world of the dead below. People often regarded illness as a punishment for their sins, or as an attack by a demon. So they were as likely to seek a cure from a priest or a magic-man as from a doctor. A stomach-ache can be painful, whatever its cause, but it makes a great deal of difference whether you view it as caused by a demon or by bacteria.

So is the ancient world and its literature – including the Bible – a closed book to us? And even if we can get inside the minds of writers from long ago, why should we take them seriously? How can biblical books from a primitive world speak to a world familiar with satellites, aircraft hijacks, computers and genetic engineering? We must acknowledge that there is a problem. Between the New Testament and us there is a gap of time, distance and culture which cannot be bridged by slick answers. But there are bridges, there are reasons for expecting that the New Testament *will* speak to us.

First, there is a real sense in which human nature does not change. Shakespeare, from four hundred years ago, and even ancient Greek playwrights from twenty-four hundred years ago, still grip people's imaginations, because they deal with great themes such as guilt, love, jealousy, justice, which we all recognize as central to human experience. For the same reason, people in many different cultures speak of the Bible not only as a book which they read, but as a book which reads them. Its exposure of human nature rings true. So when Jesus speaks of the evil which comes out of people's hearts (Mark 7.20–23), we see something of ourselves described there. When Pilate, at the trial of Jesus, hovers between the demands of truth and of political expediency (John 18.28 to 19.16), we understand the dilemma he faces.

Secondly, it *is* possible to enter imaginatively into the world of the past and the thoughts of people who lived there. Stand among tourists in an ancient building, or visit the Viking Centre in York, and you see scores of people entering into another culture. It is not only the strangeness they notice, but also the links which bind us to our past. But to understand that world of the past, you have to listen to it, giving opportunity for it to reveal its own viewpoint, rather than assuming that its viewpoint will be the same as yours. A friend who studied in Nigeria said he had to learn how Nigerians understand time differently from Europeans or Americans. An African's life is structured by events, not by watches. For example, in the West a wedding may be set for three o'clock, and everything is organized to fit that timing. If at five minutes past three the bride has not arrived, the wedding will be late. But in Nigeria the wedding will take place in the afternoon. 'It is the event that gives time its meaning and the time of the wedding will be determined by when the bride and groom arrive and the service takes place. Therefore in the African understanding of time it is not possible for the service to be late.' You can understand another culture, if you listen and look for clues.

Thirdly, the distance between us and the New Testament is not an uninhabited desert. We are linked to the first christians by a continuous stream of christian life and faith. We understand the New Testament, not like an archaeologist trying to decipher a newly discovered text, but in the context of a christian community which has been grappling with and living by these scriptures ever since they were written. And of course we are linked to Jesus, the central focus of the New Testament, not *merely* through reading about him, but also through a living experience of him. So we are never simply trying to recapture a bygone world. We are studying the writings of people who were closely linked with the historical Jesus, in order to understand and encounter more fully the risen Jesus.

The world of the New Testament

We have seen the importance of entering imaginatively into the world of the New Testament, if we are to understand its message. Learning about the *context* in which something is written helps to safeguard us against misunderstanding its significance. Take, for example, Winston Churchill's words, 'I have nothing to offer but blood, toil, tears and sweat'. To appreciate their significance we have to know that Churchill was speaking in the early dark days of the Second World War, shortly before the evacuation from Dunkirk. It is the same with Jesus' enigmatic words, 'Pay to the Emperor what belongs to him, and pay to God what belongs to God' (Mark 12.17). We need to know something of Jesus' political and religious context if we are to grasp what Jesus meant, and what the saying might imply for us. So the rest of this chapter will offer a bird's eye view of the world in which the New Testament appeared. And we shall see examples of how light is shed on New Testament passages by this kind of understanding.

Through most of their history, the experience of the jewish people has been an experience of subjection to foreign powers. From the sixth century BC Palestine was part of the Persian Empire. But between 334 and 327 BC the whole of this vast empire, stretching from Turkey in the west to the borders of India in the east, fell to Alexander the Great of Macedon. When Alexander died in 323 BC his empire was divided between his generals, so Palestine was ruled first from Egypt and then, after 200 BC from Syria. The importance of the upheavals brought by Alexander and his successors, is that they brought with them Greek language and culture, which eventually led to open confrontation in Palestine.

Under the Syrian ruler Antiochus Epiphanes (175–163 BC), things came to a head. Already some jews had been enthusiastic about Greek education and Greek styles of architecture were being imitated in Palestine. Jewish young men began to turn up in the newly-built gymnasium in Jerusalem in the fashionable dress of Athenian youth. Even priests were such keen spectators at the athletic fields, that some would leave the altar of sacrifice in the temple and rush to see the discus-throwing when they heard the starting-signal (see 2 Maccabees 4.14, in the Apocrypha)! Imagine how traditional jews were scandalized by the introduction of athletics which, by Greek custom, was performed naked. But worse was to come. Antiochus infuriated jews by auctioning off the office of high priest to the highest bidder and by plundering the temple with his army. He ordered the outlawing of the jewish religion. Mothers who had their sons circumcized were to be put to death; copies of the Law were to be burned. Jews were forced to offer sacrifice to the Greek god Zeus and to eat pigs' flesh.

In 167 BC an altar of Zeus was erected in the temple and pigs were sacrificed on it. Smouldering resentment among jews led to outright rebellion – the 'Maccabaean

Revolt', led by an old priest named Mattathias and then by his five sons, particularly Judas Maccabaeus. Syrian armies were no match for their guerrilla tactics, and in 164 Judas was able to purify the temple – an event celebrated ever since by jews at the festival of Hanukkah. Eventually, in 143 BC, the jews were set free from Syrian rule, and were an independent nation for the next eighty years. The story of the confrontation between Greek culture, especially as it was imposed by Antiochus, and jewish tradition, is told in the Apocrypha in 1 and 2 Maccabees. It is important because it made a deep impression on the minds of jews for many decades afterwards. Perhaps one reason why Pharisees were so hostile to Jesus' liberal attitude to the sabbath, was the memory that their ancestors had died for their faithfulness to the sabbath law.

Sadly, jewish rulers during this period of independence were frequently corrupt, and Greek influence continued to increase. In 63 BC the power of Rome extended its grip to Palestine, and rulers of Judea, such as the half-jewish Herod the Great (40–4 BC), reigned only by permission of the Roman Senate.

Subjects of the Roman Empire

Those eighty years from 143 to 63 BC, were the only years between 587 BC and AD 1948 when the jews were a self-governing nation. But how did Rome come to be a world power? Originally a small city-state, it had gradually gained control over surrounding countries from the third century BC, and within two hundred years it ruled all the lands surrounding the Mediterranean. But control over subject peoples requires armies, and armies have generals who aspire to ever-increasing power. So in the first century before Christ Rome experienced constant upheaval as generals bidding for supreme power led their armies into battle against other Roman generals. Julius Caesar was assassinated in 44 BC by people who suspected him of trying to become a dictator. His heir, Octavian, along with Mark Antony, avenged his death. Then Octavian and Mark Antony fought for power until Octavian won a sea battle in 31 BC, when Mark Antony sailed off to Egypt and to Cleopatra. But chased by Octavian, Mark Antony committed suicide, and thus left Octavian as the most powerful man in the world.

Octavian took the name Augustus, and became the first Roman emperor. The old aristocratic method of government through the senate remained, in theory, but the real power lay with Augustus because he controlled the armies and held all the important offices of state. But the people of Rome were in no mood to complain about that. They acclaimed Augustus as 'saviour of the world' because at last continual conflict had given way to peace and stability. Augustus held power till his death in AD 14, and so is mentioned in Luke 2.1 as the emperor at the time of Jesus' birth. He was succeeded by Tiberius (AD 14–37), emperor during Jesus' ministry (Luke 3.1).

Most Romans saw the empire as a good thing. It meant power, trade, prosperity, security. But Rome's subjects in Judea saw things very differently. To them the Roman empire meant government imposed on them against their will. When Herod the Great died in 4 BC Augustus shared his kingdom among Herod's three sons. Herod Antipas received Galilee in the north and remained its ruler till after Jesus' ministry (see Luke 3.1; 23.6–12). Herod Philip got north-eastern Palestine, including what we call the Golan Heights. Archelaus was given the prize territory, Judea and Samaria, but he made a mess of it and in AD 6 was deposed and replaced by a governor (procurator or praefectus) appointed directly by the emperor. Pontius Pilate (governor AD 26–36) lacked political judgement and infuriated jews by provocative acts. For example, he sent troops into Jerusalem by night, bearing standards inscribed with Roman images – an insensitive act in violation of the first commandment which bans the making of any carved image.

For jewish subjects the empire also meant soldiers, armies constantly available to impose Rome's will and to crush dissidents. A revolt in AD 6 led by Judas the Galilean was quickly squashed, and three thousand rebels were crucified along the roadside as a grim deterrent to others. In the Sermon on the Mount Jesus says, 'If one of the occupation troops forces you to carry his pack one kilometre, carry it two kilometres' (Matthew 5.41). Set that in the context of a nation seething with resentment at an occupying power, and you have some idea how shocking Jesus' teaching was.

Worst of all, perhaps, Roman occupation meant taxes which could be very burdensome in a land which was unlikely to produce more crops than were required for subsistence. Hatred was focused both on the Roman authorities and on the jewish tax-collectors through whose traitorous hands the taxes passed on their way to the Roman treasuries.

No wonder that hopes of a Messiah were alive among the jews of Palestine. The hoped-for Messiah would deliver them from foreign oppression, as Judas Maccabaeus and his brothers had done a few generations earlier, and establish God's rule of peace, freedom and justice as the prophets had promised. It would be wrong, however, to imagine that all jews of Jesus' time shared the same beliefs about the Messiah or about many other things. There were four distinct groups which may be mentioned.

Jewish religious groups

The sadducees belonged mostly to the priestly aristocracy, and stood to preserve their wealth and power by keeping in favour with Rome. Though opponents would accuse them of collaborating with Rome out of pure self-interest, they would see themselves as political realists, and sometimes sadducees did defend jewish interests against Roman insensitivity or incompetence. They were conservative in their beliefs. Because they gave supreme authority only to the first five books of the Bible – the law – they had no clear Messianic hope, or belief in resurrection of the dead. Hence their cynical question to Jesus in Mark 12.18–27: if a woman marries seven brothers in turn, each one dying childless so that, according to the law, the next brother is obliged to marry her, whose wife will she be in the resurrection?

The pharisees took seriously their calling to practise and to teach the law. Generally respected by the people, they tried to apply the law of Moses to the details of everyday life. They developed a body of oral law to explain and apply the written law of the Old Testament. For example, they taught people how to keep the sabbath holy (Exodus 20.8) by providing a list of what kinds of work were forbidden on the sabbath. Strict observance of the law would pave the way for the coming of the Messiah. Unlike the sudducees, they believed in the resurrection of the dead. Paul, a pharisee himself, turned this disagreement to his own advantage when questioned by the Sanhedrin in Jerusalem. (The Sanhedrin was the council of senior jewish statesmen, composed mainly of sadducees, but also of pharisees.) 'I am a pharisee,' he said. "I am on trial here because I hope that the dead will be raised to life!' As a result sadducees and pharisees argued fiercely among themselves, the pharisees taking Paul's side (Acts 23.6–10).

In the gospels the pharisees get a bad press, because their concern for the details of the law could make them blind to the big demands of caring about the sick and needy (see Matthew 9.13; 23.23). But not everything was bad about the pharisees. Their instincts were right. They were concerned to defend genuine religious values. Once some pharisees were helpful enough to warn Jesus of Herod Antipas' plot to kill him (Luke 13.31). It was a pharisee, Nicodemus, who came seeking truth from Jesus and helped in his burial (John 3.1; 19.39–42).

A group known to us from the Dead Sea Scrolls are the essenes. They interpreted the law even more rigorously than the pharisees. Their community at Qumran by the Dead Sea existed to 'prepare a way for the Lord in the wilderness' (Isaiah 40.3). In their monastic life they observed the law, studied the scriptures and their scrolls, waiting for the coming of God's kingdom. Although they are not mentioned in the New Testament, the essenes are an example of jews in Jesus' time who fervently expected the day of the Lord to come soon. They in fact believed that God's kingdom would be established after a final battle in which they themselves would defeat God's enemies, including the Romans and the corrupt Jerusalem priesthood.

Whereas the essenes were prepared to wait until God gave the signal for the final battle to begin, the zealots were a group of revolutionaries eager to take the nation's destiny into their own hands. There had been spasmodic revolts already during Jesus' lifetime. But as resentment at the Roman occupation increased, terrorist activities became commonplace. Jews who collaborated with the Romans were taken hostage, or stabbed in crowded streets. Then in AD 66 full-scale revolt broke out. Zealots took over the temple and proclaimed Jerusalem's freedom. In Galilee armed bands attacked Roman forces. It took the Roman legions four years to crush the rebellion.

In AD 70, after a long siege, the temple was the last part of Jerusalem to be captured. It was destroyed by fire and hundreds of jews of all ages were butchered. There was no Maccabaean deliverance this time, no Messiah to overthrow God's enemies.

The fall of Jerusalem and destruction of the temple was a crucial turning-point in the story of the jews. It marked the end of worship at the temple, and the end of their presence as a nation in Palestine until 1948. Jesus had, in fact, warned that the nation was heading for disaster (Mark 13.14–19). But who in AD 30 could have predicted that of all the religious groups found within Judaism, the two to survive for twenty centuries would be the pharisees – who shaped Judaism's development after AD 70 – and the followers of Jesus? Sadducees and zealots were discredited by the events which we have just surveyed, and the essenes disappeared into the desert sand.

The Church in the Greek and Roman world

That was the world in which the infant church in Palestine began to grow – a world of increasing tension as the nation lurched towards its confrontation with Rome. But elsewhere the Church was already taking root in the very different soil of Greek and Roman society.

A missionary, such as Paul, was able to travel from city to city, often using the roads which had been developed for swift movement of Roman armies. He had no language problems, since Greek was spoken all round the Eastern Mediterranean and even in Italy itself. But he had to relate his message to the culture and attitudes, the hopes and fears of these Gentile city people. We may guess from literature of the time what were some of their typical concerns.

Juvenal, a satirical poet a few decades after Paul, suggests that materialism was rife.

> The most popular, urgent prayer, well-known in every temple, is for wealth. 'Increase my holdings, please make my deposit account the largest in town!'

For many ordinary men, pleasure was what made life worth living. An inscription says:

> Wine, women and the baths corrupt our bodies;
> But what is it that makes life worth living?
> Wine, women and the baths!

Gladiatorial shows, athletic games and chariot racing attracted huge crowds, and emperors and provincial governors laid on such spectacles to win popularity among the masses.

But there was also a searching for answers to life's mysteries. The sadness of death often surfaces, as in the Roman poet, Catullus, in the first century BC:

> Suns may set and rise again;
> When once our brief life has set
> One unbroken night remains.

Many people turned to magic or astrology to find their way through life. Colourful secret cults from the east, known as mystery religions, claimed to offer immortality and freedom from guilt. More serious people looked to philosophy in their search for truth and the right way to live.

First century people were real people, ordinary people. Their faces can still be seen on wall-paintings at Pompeii. Their family letters can still be read, preserved for two thousand years in rubbish dumps in the dry sands of Egypt. To catch a glimpse of their world is to understand a little better what the message of Paul and other missionaries would mean for them. We shall see especially in chapter four how an awareness of that world will help us towards discovering what the message means for us.

Summary

In this chapter we have seen the impact which the New Testament makes on people's lives, as well as the strangeness of it which sometimes puzzles us. We have learnt the importance of understanding the New Testament in its context, and so we have surveyed the historical and religious context in which it arose. Our survey was not meant to be comprehensive, but simply to catch the atmosphere. We could have considered, also, how geography affects our understanding of a passage: it helps, when you read the parable of the Good Samaritan (Luke 10.25–37) to know what the road was like from Jerusalem to Jericho; and in chapter four we shall notice how the geographical position of Corinth affected the life of the city and made the life of the church difficult.

But we have seen enough now to recognize some of the questions which we need to ask of a New Testament passage:

What is its historical context?

What religious issues or arguments does it reflect?

Do geographical factors affect our understanding of it?

Can we enter imaginatively into the thought-worlds and attitudes of people who feature in the passage?

Questions for discussion

Note: These questions are only suggestions. Some groups will find other questions and study ideas more helpful.

See the end of chapter ten for information about study aids and commentaries. A group leader who wishes to use the following questions may want first to invite group members to raise questions which have come to mind through their reading of this chapter.

1 *Why* do you think the New Testament sometimes affects people in the way described at the beginning of this chapter? Can you share any similar stories from your own experience or from the experience of people you know?

2 What seems to you to be the biggest difficulties about understanding the New Testament? Are there some ways in which you find its message remote from twentieth century life? Be honest! Members of the group may like to share ideas about how to overcome these difficulties, or you may wish to make a note of them and look for answers as you continue studying this book.

3 Has the information given in this chapter about the world of Jesus and of the first christians shed light on your understanding of any particular passage or problem in the New Testament? How?

4 Study John 4.1–26. How can our understanding of it be helped by asking such questions as:

What religious issues or arguments does it reflect?

Do geographical factors affect our understanding of it?

Can we enter imaginatively into the longings of many of Jesus' contemporaries for a Messiah, a deliverer? If you were a first-century jew or samaritan, would you feel that Jesus fulfilled those longings?

2

The gospels – four portraits of Jesus

'There's nothing like a good story', we say. Whether it is *Dallas* or *Oliver Twist* or *The Three Billy-Goats Gruff*, we humans find stories more appealing than other forms of expression. Unlike a philosophical lecture or a scientific report, a story draws us in, makes us sympathize with the characters, holds us in suspense. As the story carries us along, we feel in turn excited, apprehensive, angry, joyful. It's no accident, then, that the central facts of christian faith are presented for us in story form. The four gospels hold Jesus before us, not as a doctrine to be analysed or a philosophy to be disputed, but as a person who evokes our interest, our wonder and our obedience.

Now we need to ask, 'What kind of a book is a gospel?' It is not enough simply to call it a story because all kinds of different things can be expressed in story form. History, biography, fictional novel, newspaper report, parable and punch-line joke are all cast in narrative or story form, but we don't treat them all in the same way. So to understand a gospel correctly, we must ask what kind of a book it is meant to be.

Most people assume that the gospels are biographies of Jesus. But they are hardly typical biographies. Take Mark, for example, which was probably the earliest gospel to be written. What kind of a biography is it that tells us nothing of Jesus' birth or childhood, or what he looked like? Why is Mark so vague about the length of Jesus' ministry or the timing of events within it? Why does the story of his approach to Jerusalem and to the cross fill the last half of Mark's book?

It is an unusual book, but not entirely different in form from anything that had been written before. In the Greek and Roman world, people wrote biographies of famous men such as Socrates, the philosopher. As well as recounting the deeds and teachings of their hero in an attractive way, they often had particular reasons for writing. They wanted to defend their hero against his critics or enemies – 'This is what our teacher was *really* like'. Or they aimed to pass on the teachings of their hero and to describe his life as an example to their readers. It is easy to see that Mark's gospel has plenty in common with those Greek biographies. He is not giving a comprehensive account of Jesus' life, but selecting events and sayings of Jesus which will demonstrate what he was like, what his mission was, what he taught, how people reacted to him.

Yet that doesn't fully explain the nature of Mark's book. For Mark, Jesus is not – like Socrates – a teacher to be revered and explained. As James Denney put it, 'No apostle, no New Testament writer, ever *remembered* Christ.' Mark was not preserving the memory of a dead hero, but proclaiming a living Lord. His gospel has to be read on two levels. On one level it is an account of what Jesus did and said during his ministry; but always there is a message on another level: this same Jesus, risen and alive, continues to act in power and to guide people's lives by his teaching. So readers see in the Jesus of the gospel the Lord of their own experience; and they see their own reactions to Jesus mirrored in the gospel's account of the disciples' faltering response, and sometimes in the reactions of the crowds and the enemies of Jesus.

Building-blocks for a gospel

Mark's gospel probably did not appear in writing till

about AD 65, more than thirty years after Jesus' ministry. Before that, christians shared their message mostly by word of mouth. Jesus himself could write, as John 8.8 shows (I wonder what he wrote!), but he didn't write his teaching down. He lived in an oral culture where most people preferred the spoken to the written word. So what prompted Mark to produce a book? Almost certainly he wrote because the apostles (who had been guardians of the stories about Jesus) were now dying through persecution or sheer old age. An ancient tradition says that Mark 'transmitted in writing those things which Peter had preached'.

We are not, however, to think of Mark sitting down, pen poised, and Peter saying to him: 'I'm going to die soon. So write some notes about my reminiscences of Jesus. I remember one day when we were in Capernaum . . .' Scholars have shown that Mark's gospel consists not of one man's reminiscences, but of stories and sayings which have been repeated continually by a wide range of preachers. During that thirty year period between Jesus' resurrection and Mark's writing, stories of Jesus were passed on by word of mouth as the Church was involved in mission, worship and teaching.

If you look at a section of Mark's gospel, such as chapters one to three, you will notice that it is made up of a number of paragraphs (each with its own heading in the *Good News Bible*). That is not remarkable in itself, of course, since all books are written in paragraphs. But unlike paragraphs in most books, each paragraph here tells a story which is complete in itself. Each paragraph makes its own point and is connected only very loosely with what comes before or after it. Mark 2.23, for example, begins: 'Jesus was walking through some cornfields on the sabbath'. We are not told which cornfields or which sabbath, or how long after the previous incident it took place. This story carries its own message, and we don't have to read the surrounding paragraphs in order to understand what that message is. This suggests to us that before the stories were written down they circulated among christians as independent units. We can imagine how a preacher would pick on this or that unit – a story or a saying of Jesus – to bring home some point in the course of his preaching. Mark's gospel is like a building constructed out of these small building-blocks, which at first existed independently of each other.

These building-blocks do not all have the same shape. In the course of frequent use in preaching they were 'streamlined' into several groups, each with its distinctive shape or form. Just as you can recognize a limerick, a wedding invitation or an advert for a house sale by the distinctive form of each, you can recognize different kinds of units in a gospel. For instance, there are 'pronouncement stories'. These are brief episodes which lead up to an authoritative saying of Jesus, or sometimes a statement about the reaction of the onlookers. Mark 2.23–28 is an example. Here the details of the incident – the disciples picking corn on the sabbath, and Jesus' argument with the pharisees – are told as briefly as possible in order to build up towards the climax: 'The sabbath was made for the good of man; man was not made for the sabbath. So the Son of Man is Lord even of the sabbath'. As in a punch-line joke, this final saying is the important thing. The rest of the paragraph only matters in that it provides the setting for Jesus' declaration about the sabbath.

Other pronouncement stories include the call of the four fishermen (Mark 1.16–20); the call of Levi (2.13–14); the question about Jesus' eating with outcasts (2.15–17); the question about fasting (2.18–22). In each case Jesus' authoritative saying or 'pronouncement' is the focus of attention. We can imagine how early preachers would use such stories in order to bring home Jesus' declared will on a controversial matter, such as the right use of the sabbath. Or to announce authoritatively his offer of salvation and summons to discipleship – 'Follow me!' This makes it clear that these stories about Jesus were remembered in the early Church not simply to preserve the memory of Jesus, but because they were *useful* for the life and mission of the Church. They were remembered because they were used, and they were used because they gave guidance, answered questions and communicated Christ to the Church and its hearers.

Miracle stories

A different category of units in the gospels is the miracle story, such as that of the healing of Simon's mother-in-law (Mark 1.29–31), or of the man with a skin disease (1.40–45). All miracle stories follow the same basic pattern: first, a description of the disease or the situation to be remedied; second, a statement of the cure or solution achieved by Jesus; third, a statement of the results of the miracle – either the effects on the person healed or the reaction of the onlookers. This is a natural pattern for any story of this kind, whether it is a New Testament healing story or a TV advert for vitamin pills or medicated shampoo. In a miracle story attention is focused not so much on a saying of Jesus as on his *power* to overcome evil and to deal with distress.

Interestingly, some stories appear to be a mixture of both pronouncement and miracle story. The stories of the paralysed man (Mark 2.1–12) and of the man with the paralysed hand (3.1–6) both report healings, yet there is little doubt that the heart of these stories lies not in the miracle itself but in the pronouncement of Jesus that accompanies it. In the first story Jesus' ability to heal serves to demonstrate his 'authority on earth to forgive sins' (2.10). In the second the real issue is not the healing itself but the question about the sabbath – is it right on the sabbath to help or to harm, to save life or to destroy it (3.6)?

Not every story in Mark's gospel can be classified as a miracle story or pronouncement story. For example, the opening paragraphs about John the Baptist and about Jesus' baptism and temptation are stories which fit no obvious category. But the first christians did not repeat these stories, either, simply to report what had happened, but to convey what *significance* those happenings had for them and their hearers.

Much of the gospels contain teaching or sayings of Jesus rather than stories about him. These take various forms. For instance, there are sayings cast in proverbial form – 'Many who now are first will be last, and many who now are last will be first' (Mark 10.31); and commands or exhortations – 'If anyone wants to come with me, he must forget self, carry his cross, and follow me' (Mark 8.34). Parables, of course, are especially characteristic of Jesus' teaching. These range from short sayings expressed in picture language – 'You must be as cautious as snakes and as gentle as doves' (Matthew 10.16) – to story parables such as the Sower (Mark 4.3–9) and the Prodigal Son (Luke 15.11–32). We shall look at parables more closely in the next chapter.

So far we have seen that Mark constructed his gospel out of short units of narrative or teaching which had been used by preachers and passed on orally for the previous thirty years. Each unit brought home some particular aspect of the good news about Jesus, and each was remembered because it was useful for the Church's life.

If all this is true, it gives us three important guidelines for interpreting passages in the gospels. First, if the traditions about Jesus were remembered because they answered questions and met needs in the life of the

Church, we can try to visualize *what* situation in the Church a particular unit was found useful for, and *how* it was useful. When the early Church and its concerns have 'come alive' for us in this way, we shall be more able to look for parallel situations in our own context, and think how the word of Jesus applies to us. For instance, if I recognize that the issue of divorce and remarriage (Mark 10.2–12) was a matter of vigorous debate among jewish teachers of Jesus' time, and an urgent question for early christians (as Paul makes clear in 1 Corinthians 7), this should help me to be thoughtful and sympathetic in relating Jesus' teaching to today's situation.

Secondly, we shall develop an instinct for focusing attention on the part of a passage where the first tellers of the story *intended* attention to be focused. For example, when studying a pronouncement story such as the story of the paralysed man (Mark 2.1–12), we shall not get side-tracked into debate as to whether it is moral to remove other people's roofs without permission. Instead, we shall concentrate on the wonder of the fact that Jesus has God-given authority to forgive sins instantly.

Lastly, we shall expect each paragraph to bring home some specific message about Jesus and our response to him, just as it did before Mark wrote it down.

Why four gospels?

It is an intriguing question. If Mark wrote his gospel around AD 65, why did anyone think it necessary to write more than one gospel? Why four? Why not three, or eight? It appears that once Mark's gospel had been written – probably for the church in Rome – it began to be copied for the benefit of christians in other places. But some evidently recognized that it was selective in its use of traditions about Jesus and didn't include stories and sayings which were precious to them. So Matthew and Luke, building on Mark's account, produced fuller versions of the gospel story. Read Luke's opening paragraph (Luke 1.1–4), and you will see him explaining how he has decided to build on earlier accounts, so as to bring home 'the full truth' for his readers.

Clearly, there is a very close relationship between the three gospels of Matthew, Mark and Luke. Many passages are found in all three gospels: paragraph headings in the *Good News Bible* show where the same material can be found in other gospels. And often the wording found in these parallel passages is so close that the similarity can only have arisen through one writer copying another. Read, for example, about Jesus' call of the four fishermen in Matthew 4.18–22, and Mark 1.16–20, or the healing story in Matthew 8.1–14, Mark 1.40–45 and Luke 5.12–16, and you can see how slight the differences are. If the gospel-writers had been writing the stories down from their own memory of hearing them preached, the variations of wording would surely have been greater.

Because they share so much material together, these first three gospels are called the 'synoptic' gospels, from the Greek *synopsis* (meaning 'seeing together'). Most scholars agree that Mark wrote first. For it is very hard to imagine why, if Matthew or Luke already existed, Mark would have bothered writing a shorter gospel *omitting* such central passages as the Sermon on the Mount and the Lord's Prayer. But there is every reason why Matthew or Luke, on reading Mark, should want to *add* such important passages. Matthew and Luke probably wrote about AD 80. They used Mark as their main source, but combined it with other material which had already been written in other documents (which do not survive). Matthew and Luke may also have included stories which no one had written down before, but which were familiar to them from the Church's preaching. They provided for their readers gospels which followed Mark's framework but gave a much fuller portrait of Jesus. Both have stories about Jesus' birth, much more of his teaching, and more stories of the appearances of the risen Christ.

John's gospel breathes a different atmosphere. He probably knew of the existence of one or more of the other gospels but did not depend on them for information. He tells far fewer incidents and uses those which he has selected as springboards for teaching on the significance of Jesus. For instance, in Mark the feeding of the five thousand is told in fifteen verses (Mark 6.30–44). But in John 6 it is developed into a chapter-long discourse and debate about Jesus as the Bread of Life. John has not, it seems, given us an unadorned report of what Jesus said after the feeding miracle. He has built on memories of what Jesus said to explain what Jesus means for him and his readers. He himself says he has selected the miracles highlighted in his gospel 'in order that you may believe that Jesus is the Messiah, the Son of God, and that through your faith in him you may have life' (John 20.31). By this he probably means that his purpose is to confirm and develop the faith which his readers already have, rather than to bring them to faith for the first time. He wrote about AD 90.

Why four gospels? Once Mark's gospel had appeared, the other three authors wanted to tell the story afresh. Although two of them depended heavily on Mark, they all aimed, by their selection and presentation of material, to relate the story of Jesus to the situation of their own readers. How they selected and presented material we shall see in chapter three. For the moment, we may simply note that once these four gospels had appeared, no one, as far as we know, wrote another one. Admittedly, early in the second century someone produced *The Gospel of Thomas*, but this is a collection of sayings, not a narrative of Jesus' ministry, death and resurrection.

And even later, other stories about Jesus were written, but these are mostly romantic tales – about his childhood, for example – and are different from the New Testament gospels.

So the four gospels are all we have. And before the end of the second century people were saying it was just as natural that there should be four gospels as that there are four points on the compass. It means that we have four presentations of Jesus, each with its own emphasis, just as four portraits of a single person emphasize different aspects of their subject's character. Mark, it has been suggested, shows us the crucified Christ, Matthew shows us Christ the teacher, Luke presents Christ as the Saviour of all people, and John proclaims the eternal Christ. That is an over-simplification, but it points in the right direction. Without any one of the gospels we would certainly be much the poorer.

Can we trust the gospels?

Before we move on to questions about how we may interpret the gospels' differing presentations of Jesus, we must face another vital question. Can we trust them? Do they give a reliable account of Jesus' ministry? Didn't exaggerations creep into the telling of the stories during those thirty years before Mark wrote? Don't the gospels contradict each other? Here are five reasons why we can have confidence in the gospel accounts.

First, thirty years is not a long time in which to remember things in a culture where stories and ideas are communicated mostly orally rather than on paper. In our western culture we forget a lot because written records remove from us the *need* to remember – just as the pocket calculator is rapidly removing the need, and therefore the ability, to do mental arithmetic. But in the first century it was different. Some Greek and Roman schoolboys could memorize books of poetry longer than the whole New Testament. In Palestine, jewish teachers memorized large blocks of legal interpretation, stories and sayings, and passed them on to their disciples. When a rabbi died it was said, 'Alas, a walking library has been lost'. His knowledge was all in his head, not in books! So there is no reason to doubt the ability of ordinary christians and their leaders to preserve accurately the traditions about Jesus. And the constant use of these traditions in preaching and worship would reinforce their memories.

Secondly, against the possibility of exaggeration or distortion there were safeguards. The presence in the church of people who had seen and heard Jesus would guard against serious distortion. And one of the chief functions of the apostles was to guarantee the truth of the traditions. For they had been with Jesus during his ministry and had witnessed his resurrection (see Acts 1.21–22). As we saw earlier, the death of apostles provoked the conclusion that the reliability of the traditions must now be safeguarded in a different way – by writing it down in gospels.

Thirdly, where the gospel accounts can be checked against other evidence, they are generally shown to be accurate in their historical references. We saw how Luke wanted to present himself as having done careful research (Luke 1.1–4), and at several points his accuracy is confirmed by non-biblical sources. Admittedly, his reference to the census under Quirinius in Luke 2.1–2 does seem at odds with the later dating given by the jewish historian Josephus. But Luke's information about secular rulers in 3.1 is confirmed by other sources, and his several references in Acts to the titles of Roman provincial governors and city officials have been confirmed by inscriptions found by archaeologists. (An array of Greek technical terms, which Luke could hardly have guessed but must have researched carefully, underlies the *Good News Bible* in Acts 13.7; 16.20; 17.6; 18.12; 19.31).

Fourthly, if people in the early Church had been inventing sayings of Jesus, we would have expected them to create sayings which dealt with issues which were of great concern or controversy among them; then they would have 'authoritative' words from Jesus about these great issues. What were some of the issues they faced in those early years after the resurrection? Two obvious examples are the dispute over whether gentiles could be admitted to the Church without circumcision, and the controversy about charismatic gifts. Yet there is not a whisper of these issues in the gospels. On the other hand, things which *are* central in the gospels, such as the use of 'Son of Man' with reference to Jesus, the term 'kingdom of God' and his use of parables, are all absent, or almost absent, from the rest of the New Testament. In other words, early christians were able to distinguish clearly between what Jesus was known to have done or said, and what was done and said within the Church's own developing life. This is further supported by the way in which Paul, in 1 Corinthians 7, makes a sharp distinction between the remembered and authoritative word of Jesus about divorce (verse 10) and his own opinion – guided by God's Spirit – on matters which the historical Jesus had not pronounced upon (verses 12, 25, 40).

The fifth point concerns miracles, which for many people raise the most serious problems. A historian who sees his job as explaining events in terms of cause and effect may well wonder how miracles can be accommodated in his historical study. For miracles involve a seemingly irrational suspension of the normal laws of cause and effect, and so are open to the gravest suspicion. However, many physicists today are saying that the world is a stranger, less predictable place than we used to think. And there is no reason why we should rule out the possibility that God's involvement with his world sometimes means his acting in a more 'direct' way than normal. The philosopher, T. E. Jessop, wrote: 'If the universe is dominated by a Spirit, miracles are possible; if by a Spirit that is love, probable; and if that Spirit has become incarnate, this miracle would make further ones very probable indeed.'

Add to this, moreover, the fact that Jesus' critics did not deny the reality of his miracles, but attributed them to Satan (Mark 3.20–29). Such an idea would hardly have been invented by the early christians, and it shows that Jesus was known for his supernatural powers. The tradition that Jesus worked miracles is also reported by Josephus, the jewish historian, and finds an echo in the later jewish theory that Jesus was a sorcerer. All this doesn't automatically prove beyond doubt that all reported miracles of Jesus are genuine. They remain mysterious, and sometimes difficult to understand. But they have a strong claim to be treated as part of the bedrock of reliable tradition.

History and John's gospel

John's gospel, as we have already seen, has to be viewed rather differently from the synoptic gospels. There is a greater measure of reflection and interpretation of what Jesus says and who he is than we find in the other gospels. This is illustrated, for example, by the fact that it is sometimes impossible to distinguish where a speech of Jesus finishes and the gospel-writer's own reflection begins. When we read that 'God loved the world so much that he gave us his only Son . . .' (John 3.16), are we reading part of Jesus' speech, or part of John's meditation on the speech which, according to the *Good News Bible*, finished at verse 14? The Greek manuscripts have no quotation marks, so every translator has to make his own judgment as to where a quotation begins and ends. Usually it is obvious, but here and in some other places in John there is no clear end to the speech. John has merged it into his own reflections on the significance of Jesus.

John also declares who Jesus is rather more explicitly than the synoptics do. In the other gospels, Jesus' claim to be in a unique relationship to God is implicit rather than explicit. In John, attention is persistently focused on the person of Jesus. A hundred times he speaks of God as his Father, and over twenty times of himself as God's Son. The 'I am' sayings declare his significance more boldly than anything in the synoptics (John 6.35; 8.12; 10.7, 11; 11.25; 14.6). If Jesus had really spoken in precisely those terms, it is hard to understand why the other gospels show no trace of such sayings.

John appears to have taken truths about Jesus which *are* present in the other gospels, and highlighted them in a way which would communicate the significance of Jesus for his readers. For instance, in the synoptics there is a parable about a shepherd who goes out searching for his lost sheep (Luke 15.4–7). In telling it Jesus implies that *his* caring for outcasts and bringing them to God is like a shepherd's care for his sheep. The Jesus of John's gospel makes this more explicit by saying, 'I am the good shepherd'. The basic message is the same, but it is expressed in a more open manner, challenging the reader to see Jesus as the focus of all God's dealings with men and women.

The fact that John seems not to have given us the exact words which Jesus used should not alarm us, once we recognize that he was not *trying* to give us, as it were, a tape-recorded account. If I want to understand the real significance of a debate in the House of Commons, I might gain *less* from tape-recorded extracts of speeches than from a report in his own words by a wise and perceptive commentator. And it is important to stress that history, to be worth anything, *must* involve interpretation. Someone might tell me that in 1974 Richard Nixon resigned the presidency of the United States. That is true, but it is a useless piece of information unless I am also offered interpretation of why it happened and what is significant about it. So the measure of interpretation which John brings to his gospel is to be welcomed, not feared.

Even so, we must not run away with the idea that John is unconcerned about what actually happened. Scholars have grown increasingly confident in recent years that he was in close touch with the places and events of Jesus' ministry. Places such as the pool of Bethesda (Bethzatha), described in John 5 are not symbolic creations of John's mind, as some people once thought. It is a real pool, a hundred yards long, excavated for all to see, in Jerusalem.

Although John's account of Jesus' ministry does not overlap a great deal with the synoptic accounts, it in fact enables us to understand some events in the synoptics which would otherwise be a mystery. For example, at the end of Mark's story of the feeding of the five thousand, we are told that Jesus made his disciples escape in a boat while he dismissed the crowd (Mark 6.45). Why? John's independent account reveals that the crowd were eager to seize him and make him king – leader of a popular uprising (John 6.15). So John's story provides the clue to explain Mark. They complement each other in a way which underlines the truth of both accounts.

These and many other details support the claim made in the gospel itself, that its account is based on eyewitness testimony (John 19.35; 21.24). The traditional view that the witness of John, 'the beloved disciple', lies behind this gospel is by no means as outlandish as has sometimes been thought.

Summary

In this chapter we have seen that the gospels are not biographies of Jesus in the normal sense. They communicate the living Christ through telling the story of the historical Jesus. We have looked at the different kinds of building-blocks which Mark took from the oral tradition for the building of his gospel. And we have seen how awareness of these building-blocks can help us to focus attention on those aspects of these passages which were most significant for the gospel-writers themselves. We have affirmed the value of having more than one portrait of Jesus in order to get a fuller picture of him and of his significance for people in different situations. Finally, we have seen that there are good reasons for believing that the gospels offer reliable accounts of Jesus' deeds and words.

Questions for discussion

1 'Mark's gospel has to be read on two levels . . .' (page 18 – read again the whole paragraph). Do you find it helpful to view the gospels in this way? Why?

2 In your experience, what reasons do people give for questioning the reliability of the gospel records? How would you respond to them?

3 Do you find yourself attracted to one of the gospels more than to the others? If so, what benefits and dangers do you think there are in having a 'favourite gospel'?

4 Study Mark 2.15–17. This is a 'pronouncement story', with the emphasis on the 'pronouncement' in verse 17. What would Jesus' 'pronouncement' mean to those who first heard it, and how would they react to it? Is it saying something to us which perhaps we find hard to hear?

3

Interpreting the gospels

If there are good reasons to trust the gospels, how are we to deal with the differences between them? What do we do when they seem to contradict each other?

Sometimes different gospels have the same material but in a different order. This can be seen by looking at the Sermon on the Mount (Matthew 5–7). Much of the teaching here is also found in Luke 6. (Compare Matthew 5.3–12 with Luke 6.20–23; Matthew 5.43–48 with Luke 6.27–36; Matthew 7.1–5 with Luke 6.37–42.) But other parts of the Sermon on the Mount are scattered elsewhere in Luke. The Lord's Prayer, for example, is in Luke 11.2–4 as well as in Matthew 6. It seems, then, that the gospel writers were not concerned to record things in correct chronological order, but often organized the material according to themes. Matthew has collected together in chapters five to seven a large amount of teaching which no doubt was originally given on a variety of occasions. This idea of grouping similar material together had already influenced Mark. He has a collection of parables in chapter four, and groups miracles together in 4.35 to 5.43.

More puzzling are the places where the gospel writers tell the same story in different ways. Why, for instance, does Luke's story of the healing of the Roman centurion's servant tell us that the centurion sent messengers to ask for Jesus' help (Luke 7.1–10), whilst Matthew says that he spoke to Jesus himself (Matthew 8.5–13)? It may help us understand this problem if we think about our daily newspapers. Read several newspapers' accounts of an important event and what do you notice? You can see that they are all reporting the same event. Parts of their stories may use almost identical words – perhaps because they are quoting from an official report or statement issued about the event. But there are differences too, which usually arise from three causes. First, one paper or another will give some information which isn't included in the other papers – perhaps because its reporter has got an exclusive interview with one of the participants. Secondly, different papers will put different 'slants' on the story because of their differing political viewpoints. Thirdly, the style of the newspapers will vary because they are aimed at different types of readers. *The Times* writes in a complicated way for complicated people, whilst *The Daily Mirror* writes more briefly and straightforwardly to communicate to straightforward people.

Similar reasons underlie differences between the gospels. We can begin to see this if we look at the story of Peter's confession at Caesarea Philippi (Matthew 16.13–23; Mark 8.27–33; Luke 9.18–22). Immediately we notice that Matthew has introduced *extra material* in comparison with Mark, his source. In verses 17–19 he has a whole new section in which Jesus declares Peter to be the rock on which the Church will be built. Presumably Matthew has access to an oral tradition which Mark did not know or chose not to use. This extra saying also reflects Matthew's special theological interest – his equivalent of the newspaper's political slant – in the nature and life of the church. Matthew is the only gospel writer (here and in 18.17), to use the word 'church'.

Luke, on the other hand, has *omitted* the episode where Peter expresses horror at the prospect of Jesus' death and Jesus rebukes him, calling him 'Satan' (Mark 8.32–33). Did Luke feel that to report this would confuse his readers, who would not be able to understand why the apostle Peter should be identified with Satan? Another interesting feature of Luke's version is that he changes Mark's 'You are the Messiah' (Mark 8.29) into 'You are God's Messiah' (Luke 9.20). A small change, but very important, perhaps, for Luke's Gentile readers. 'Messiah', meaning 'Anointed One', was a religious idea familiar to jews but baffling to gentiles. The only kind of 'anointing' of which most gentiles were aware was when they went to the public baths and had olive oil rubbed on them by the masseur. So by adding the single word 'God's', Luke makes clear that the term 'Anointed' is being used with *religious* significance. Only by using *different* words can he communicate the *same* essential message to a different audience. This shows clearly that differences between the gospels do not arise because the writers make arbitrary changes or are unconcerned about truth. Quite the opposite.

Different slants, same story

Now let's pursue a little further this question of different theological emphases in the gospels, by going back to the healing of the centurion's servant (Matthew 8.5–13; Luke 7.1–10). If you look at the two accounts side by side you can see that the crucial conversation between Jesus and the centurion (or his representatives) is almost identical in both. Both stress that it was a gentile whom Jesus commended. But was it the centurion (as Matthew has it), or his friends (Luke), who spoke to Jesus? Perhaps Matthew, in shortening the story, omitted what he regarded as a secondary detail. But certainly this and some other differences between Matthew and Luke have the effect of giving different angles or emphases to the story in their two accounts.

Luke is stressing the centurion's *humility*. Hence he sends messengers to Jesus rather than going himself, and his message is 'I do not deserve to have you come into my house, neither do I consider myself worthy to come to you in person' (verses 6–7 – the latter half of the sentence is not in Matthew). Matthew, however, focuses attention on the centurion's *faith*. He alone has Jesus' concluding words, 'Go home, and what you believe will be done for you' (verse 13). And between this and the earlier saying, 'I have never found anyone in Israel with faith like this' (verse 10), he sandwiches a passage about membership of God's kingdom (verses 11–12). This saying occurs in a quite different place in Luke (13.28–30), which suggests that Jesus did not actually utter it on the occasion of his healing of the centurion's servant. But Matthew has included it here because it underlines the fact that, since entry to the kingdom of God is through faith, it is open to gentiles, yet closed to any jews who rely on tradition rather than on faith.

So we have here a story in which Matthew and Luke agree about the central point, but bring out different secondary points. They aren't contradicting each other or straining the story. The story itself is rich and flexible enough to carry these different interpretations. Small differences like this contribute to the distinctiveness of the portrait of Jesus which each gospel, taken as a whole, presents.

A further example of different emphases is the beatitudes. Matthew 5.3–12 has the more familiar version, beginning, 'Happy are those who know they are spiritually poor; the kingdom of Heaven belongs to them!'

In comparison with Matthew's nine beatitudes, Luke has only four, beginning, 'Happy are you poor; the kingdom of God is yours!' (Luke 6.20–23). But to his four beatitudes Luke adds four 'woes' which are a mirror image of the four beatitudes (verses 24–26). So both gospel writers are drawing on a common tradition, but each adds to it other sayings, perhaps spoken by Jesus on different occasions. These different *selections* of material, together with the different *wording* of the beatitudes they share in common, results in different emphases.

So what do we make of the different versions of the first beatitude? We may be tempted to suggest that Matthew's phrase, 'those who know they are spiritually poor', indicates what Luke 'really means' by 'you poor'. But Luke can hardly have understood it this way. His contrast between blessings for the poor and woes for the rich suggests that he saw Jesus as addressing people who were literally poor. His disciples have given up everything to follow him, and he is assuring them that all the riches of God's kingdom are theirs. Matthew, by contrast, has a different slant on it. In his version the saying stresses that any of us who acknowledge our emptiness to God will be filled with the gift of his kingdom. Now *both* these emphases are God's word to us. This is what it means to take seriously the four gospels. We do not pick the version we prefer and ignore the other. We listen to Jesus saying through Matthew that we must recognize our emptiness and be open to God to fill us. And we listen to him reminding us through Luke that the God of the Bible is concerned for the poor, the forgotten, the powerless.

This brings us to one further point about the way the gospel writers have put their books together. We have seen that each writer has his own God-given insights, his own way of telling the story. A characteristic of Luke's way of telling the story is his emphasis on Jesus' particular concern for the poor, the outcasts, samaritans and gentiles – people on whom other jews would tend to look down. He does this partly by the way he *presents* the material which he shares with other gospel writers, as we have seen in the case of the beatitudes. He also does it by introducing other sayings and stories which are special to his gospel. Think, for example, of Mary's song (Luke

1.46–55), the parable of the Good Samaritan (10.30–37), the story of Zacchaeus the despised tax-collector (19.1–10), or of Jesus' sermon in the synagogue at Nazareth, where he shows how God's love reaches out to gentiles (4.16–30). All these episodes appear only in Luke, and they illustrate just one facet of Jesus' purpose to which he especially draws attention.

One of the joys of reading a particular gospel is noticing the special insights into Jesus which this writer's way of telling the story brings home. This is one reason why it is valuable sometimes to read a gospel *as a whole* – to read straight through a gospel in one or two sittings. I often ask students to read Mark's gospel straight through at the beginning of a course on the gospels. They usually surprise themselves with the things they notice which they've never seen through reading only short sections. Seeing the gospel whole brings them a fresh, sharper impression of Jesus and of the aspects of his character and message on which Mark especially focuses. And of course, after that their reading of a short section of Mark means more because they begin to see how it fits into Mark's overall purpose.

Interpretation involves asking the right questions

We can now summarize the guidelines for interpreting a passage, which are implied in our discussion so far. Bible study involves developing the art of *asking the right questions*. And we must ask *what it meant* for the gospel writer and his readers before we ask *what it means* for us. If we do not listen to what its author meant a passage to say, we shall be in too much danger of making it mean what we always thought it meant, or what we hope it means in order to confirm our own pet themes or prejudices.

Questions to ask about *what a passage meant* include:

1 *What is its context?* This question itself needs breaking down into two. First, what religious, historical, geographical and cultural context does it reflect? This was the subject of chapter one. So, for example, when we study the parable of the Good Samaritan (Luke 10.30–37), our questions will include:

What was the Jerusalem–Jericho road like? (Answer: lonely, very suitable for robbers!)

What function did priests and levites perform, and what was their position in society? (Answer: they were respected as people with religious duties to perform at the temple in Jerusalem. Perhaps the two in this story avoided helping the man because they believed that if they touched him and he was in fact dead, they would be religiously 'unclean'. But perhaps they just feared the reappearance of the robbers.)

Who were the samaritans and how did jews view them? (Answer: they lived in Samaria, between Judea in the south and Galilee in the north, and were despised by jews because they were of mixed jewish and foreign blood.)

The second question about a passage's context is: What is its context in the gospel? Why does it come at this particular point in the story, and how does it relate to the rest of the gospel? We have already seen the value of asking how the theme of a passage may relate to a gospel writer's special emphases. Awareness of a passage's relationship to other parts of the gospel will often help us avoid misinterpreting it.

One example of this is Jesus' words at the last supper: 'Whoever has no sword must sell his coat and buy one . . .' The disciples said, 'Look! Here are two swords, Lord!' 'That is enough!' he replied (Luke 22.36–38). Taken on its own, this puzzling passage might appear to suggest that Jesus encouraged violent resistance against Rome. But that option is ruled out once we study it in relation to other sayings in Luke's gospel. There is no hint of nationalism in Jesus' teaching; people he cared about included a Roman centurion (Luke 7.1–10), and when told about Pilate's cruelty to some Galileans he did not respond with a tirade about Roman atrocities (Luke 13.1–5). Moreover, the temptation story (Luke 4.1–12) shows him resisting the temptation to win the world by political or military means.

So in this passage Jesus contrasts the simple expectancy of the disciples on their first mission (see Luke 22.35, with 9.3; 10.4) with the intensity of the opposition which they are about to face. Jesus' words must be grimly ironical – if only we could hear his tone of voice! For what use would a couple of swords be against the band who will soon arrest him? Exasperated with the disciples' failure to understand, he breaks off the conversation. 'Enough of that', he says. Soon in Gethsemane a disciple would offer futile resistance by cutting off the ear of the high priest's servant with his sword. And Jesus would show *his* attitude by restoring it to health (Luke 22.49–51). Thus we see how a little exploration round Luke's gospel provides a secure framework within which we can interpret an awkward passage properly.

2 *What is its content?* Once we have asked about the context of a passage, we can study its content. This involves looking at individual words, sentences, and the passage as a whole. Words can be slippery things, they can have different meanings in different contexts. The word 'save' means different things according to whether you are at a football match, at the building society or in church. So we can't assume that a word will always mean the same in any context. Once we realize this, we shall find some puzzles are solved. Look, for instance, at John 5 where Jesus says that God the Father 'has given the Son the right to judge' (verse 27). Yet he also says that the believer in Jesus 'will not be judged' (verse 24). In verse 27

'judge' means to pass a verdict on people's lives and determine their destinies (see verses 28–29). But in verse 24 'he will not be judged' means he will not be *condemned* at the judgment. An apparent contradiction is resolved when we see that the word 'judge' is being used in two quite common but different senses.

Sentences, too, need thoughtful handling. Suppose I am studying Jesus' encounter with the rich man in Luke 18.18–30. I reach the sentence, 'It is much harder for a rich person to enter the kingdom of God than for a camel to go through the eye of a needle' (verse 25). Having found out what the words – especially 'kingdom of God' – mean, I must consider the sentence as a whole. We are sometimes told that there was a small gate in Jerusalem called the 'Needle's Eye', which a camel could squeeze through only by kneeling. But actually there never was such a gate. The whole idea is the figment of a commentator's imagination. Jesus is not saying that it's difficult for a rich man to squeeze into the kingdom. He is saying it's as *impossible* for anyone who trusts in riches to enter the kingdom, as it is for a camel to go through a needle's eye.

Once I have understood the shocking nature of that statement, I can see how the paragraph as a whole develops. For it leads to Jesus' assertion that, though it takes a miracle to bring a rich person to God, it's a miracle that God can do: 'What is impossible for man is possible for God' (verse 27).

3 *What is its significance for us?* Only when we have understood what Jesus or the author *meant*, can we ask what the passage means for us. Otherwise we may read meanings into the text which God never put there. But how do we learn the passage's significance for us once its original meaning is clear?

We keep asking questions about what *principles* are expressed in the passage, which we can apply in a similar situation. This will sometimes mean that we don't take a statement at face value. For instance, Jesus' command to the rich man to sell all his possessions and give to the poor (Luke 18.22) can hardly be an instruction for all christians to follow: such a radical demand was evidently not made of Zacchaeus (Luke 19.1–10), and Luke tells us that Jesus was for some time grateful for the resources of several wealthy women (8.3). But it *is* a challenge to all of us about the peril of seeking security in possessions rather than in God. And for some, as for the rich man who met Jesus, it may come to a straight choice between God and money.

The significance for us of a passage will vary according to *our context*. Thus Mary's Song (Luke 1.46–55) may come as a disturbing rebuke to self-satisfied Westerners, whilst being a message of hope to those who cling to existence in a shanty town outside Rio de Janeiro.

We shall think again in chapters seven to nine about how passages in the gospels apply to us. But the final part of this chapter will look at that most distinctive feature of Jesus' teaching; his use of parables.

'The Kingdom of God is like this'

Jesus was the supreme story-teller. No one else in history is remembered as the creator of so many parables of such arresting quality. They were his characteristic method of proclaiming the kingdom of God. Yet, sadly, history is littered with examples of christians misinterpreting the parables, reading their own meanings into the text rather than listening to what the text is saying.

Around AD 200, the theologian Origen explained the parable of the Good Samaritan like this:

> The man who fell among thieves is Adam. As Jerusalem represents heaven, so Jericho, to which the traveller journeyed, is the world. The robbers

> are man's enemies, the devil and his assistants. The priest stands for the Law, the Levite for the prophets. The Good Samaritan is Christ himself. The beast on which the wounded man was set, is Christ's body, which bears the fallen Adam. The inn is the Church. The two pence are the Father and the Son. The Samaritan's promise to come again is Christ's second advent.

We may smile at that, but why is it wrong? It is wrong because a doctrinal scheme has been imposed on the story when there is no clue within the story that such a scheme is intended. As if to prove this point, other theologians of the early Church imposed on the story other doctrinal schemes which were equally arbitrary.

To get to grips with the parables, we should note first that there are two main types. Some are 'example stories'. For instance, Jesus urges people to count the cost before becoming his disciples, by citing the case of a builder who will not start to build a tower without checking he can afford to complete it (Luke 14.28–30). He tells the story of the Rich Fool to illustrate the folly of piling up riches whilst ignoring God (Luke 12.13–21). Such stories are not difficult to interpret because they make their point by appealing to human experience and common sense.

The 'story parable' is more tricky. There is a superb example in the Old Testament – the parable which the prophet Nathan told to David after he had taken Bathsheba from her husband Uriah. He told of a rich man, owner of many cattle, and a poor man who had only one little lamb which he loved as a member of the family. When visitors came to the rich man's home, he didn't want to kill one of his own animals, so he took the poor man's lamb and served it up. Hearing this, David was furious with the rich man and said, 'I swear by the living

Lord that the man who did this ought to die!' And Nathan said to David, 'You are that man' (2 Samuel 12.1–7).

Now how does that story work? It creates a situation and draws the hearer into it. It makes him take sides. Then it hits him between the eyes. There is no escape from its challenge, once the hearer has been drawn in and has commited himself to a viewpoint about the characters in the story. Many of Jesus' parables work like that. They draw you into a situation, a world of thought, invite you to identify with someone in the story. And then some surprise, some twist in the tail turns your expectations upside-down.

The Labourers in the Vineyard (Matthew 20.1–16) is an instance of this. The scene is typical of Palestine in Jesus' day; labourers are hired daily to help with the harvest. The owner agrees at the beginning to pay a silver coin, the regular daily wage, but he goes on calling in extra workers at various hours of the day, and when wages are paid out at the end of the day he begins by paying the full day's wage to the late arrivals who only worked one hour. We don't have to be experts on first-century economics to sympathize with the reactions of the other workers. 'It's unfair', we shout with them, 'if those who have worked all day aren't to get more than these late-comers.' But that's the shock of the parable. 'Don't I have the right to do as I wish with my own money?' asks the owner. 'Or are you jealous because I am generous?' So the point hits home: God does not deal with people on the basis of fairness and human achievement, but on the basis of his own extravagant generosity. But the message is *conveyed* far more effectively in the parable than in my tidy one-sentence summary of its 'point'.

Now, our problem so often with the parables is that we miss that sense of shock, of a world being turned upside-down, because we do not understand how the original audience would have received the story. We may be unaware of what significance certain elements in the story had for them. For example, the story of the Ten Girls (Matthew 25.1–13) would yield its sense to us more easily if we knew a little of marriage customs in Palestine. Or a parable may fall flat for us because we already know, or think we know, what it is getting at. Thus we hear the parable of the Pharisee and the Tax-collector (Luke 18.9–14) with no sense of surprise or outrage because *we* already know that pharisees are 'baddies', examples of religious hypocrisy. But for its first audience, the parable was shocking, even outrageous, because it compared a pharisee – a respected religious leader – unfavourably with a despised tax-collector.

This is all a bit like telling jokes. If you've heard it before, its impact is lessened when you hear it again. But a joke isn't funny at all to someone who doesn't understand the significance of key characters or items in the story. I can laugh at a joke about an Englishman, an Irishman and a Scotsman, because their world is familiar to me. But the joke would have no impact in Papua New Guinea, because there the hearer has no reference-point to enable him to understand the allusions.

So if we are serious about the parables there is no escape from asking questions about the world of Jesus, the significance of the characters he refers to, the social customs mentioned in the story. And we must notice what audience a parable is addressed to. That is something the gospel writers usually tell us, and it will give us clues as to what Jesus was driving at in telling each particular story.

A good example here is the group of parables in Luke 15 – the Lost Sheep, the Lost Coin, and the Lost Son. Luke's introduction shows us *why* Jesus told these parables: pharisees and teachers of the law were complaining, 'This man welcomes outcasts and even eats with them' (Luke 15.2). So in these parables Jesus is defending against critics his message of the forgiving and accepting grace of God towards sinners. Once we see that, it will help us to grasp where the main point lies in the story of the Lost Son. For there the real focus of attention is not on the career of the son. It is on the contrast between the loving welcome of the father, who represents God, and the churlish reaction of the elder brother, who stands for Jesus' critics. In their unsympathetic attitude to the plight of the outcast, they are dangerously out of touch with God.

Getting the point of the parables

After we have explored the story, its background and its audience, in order to understand what Jesus is getting at, we have one further task. We must 'translate' it. We must find a way of retelling the story, which will convey the same truth and create the same impact as the original story. Certainly, if we are to communicate the message of a parable to others, to report our researches into its background can be as unhelpful as explaining a joke. So we must think what an audience parallel to Jesus' audience would be, and how we can convey a parallel message to them.

In the parable of the Pharisee and the Tax-collector (Luke 18.9–14), the modern parallel to the pharisee must be someone who is confident of his own religious superiority. But he must also be someone, like the pharisee, who is respected as a religious leader. The modern equivalent of the tax-collector must at least be someone despised as a parasite, an undesirable in society. So I have sometimes told the story of the Vicar and the Tramp . . . This is not to say all vicars are self-righteous hypocrites, any more than all pharisees were. But it creates the surprise, as Jesus' story did. In this way, those of us who find security in our religious status and our good works are challenged as to our attitude towards people outside our respectable circle.

There is a modern dramatised version of the Good Samaritan called 'The Parable of the Good Punk Rocker', by Paul Burbridge and Murray Watts. At one performance in a Sunday evening service, the woman at the end of our pew jumped and groaned in horror when the punk rocker appeared to tend the victim's wounds. Probably for the first time in her life the story had hit her as it hit its first hearers. It pressed home the question, 'Who is my neighbour?'

It is a good exercise for a group to write modern versions of some of the parables. They may be written by individuals or by groups of two or three. They may be written as stories or as simple dramatic sketches. They must follow the guidelines we have explored here: having discovered the original context and thrust of Jesus' story, create a story with a parallel message for a parallel audience. Some of the group's products should be good enough to share with a wider audience. And working on them will certainly help people get inside Jesus' meaning. Here is one attempt to convey in dramatic form Jesus' message about the seed which fell among thorns (Mark 4.7):

Cast: Adviser, Businessman, Vicar.

The Businessman *and the* Vicar *are sitting on chairs on different sides of the stage, the lights are up on the* Businessman, *the* Vicar *is unlit and in a freeze. Enter* Adviser.

BUSINESSMAN: Ah yes, glad to see you. Want to talk to someone about *life*, what it means. [Phone rings] Excuse me. Hello. Yes . . . yes . . . yes . . . no . . . yes,

I'll have a thousand at four-and-a-half per cent. [Puts phone down] Right, now where was I?

ADVISER: You were starting to tell me about wanting to talk about life and what it means.

BUSINESSMAN: Yes, that's it. Not sure, don't you know, what it's all about. Sometimes I find myself wondering. [Phone rings] Excuse me again. Hello. Yes . . . no . . . no . . . Listen, I told you last week that I don't want to buy British Leyland with or without Land Rover! [Puts phone down]

ADVISER: Who do you have time for in your life?

BUSINESSMAN: Well you know what they say: the devil makes work for idle hands, so I try to keep myself fairly busy, not a lot of spare time. [Phone rings] Sorry. Excuse me again. Hello. Yes . . . Thursday at two . . . yes, that's okay. I can give you twenty minutes then, but no longer than that. [Puts phone down] Sorry about that – my daughter's psychoanalyst. What were you saying?

ADVISER: You must stop and *listen*. Slow down. You're doing too much.

Lights fade on Businessman, *who freezes. Lights come up on* Vicar. Adviser *walks over to* Vicar.

VICAR: I'm glad to see you. I find our talks helpful.

ADVISER: That's good. How have things been over the past few months?

VICAR: I seem to be going through something of a dry patch spiritually. [Phone rings] Excuse me. Hello. Yes . . . Er no, I'm afraid that I'll be tied up that night with a confirmation class, but it usually finishes at half eight. I could be round by just before nine . . . Okay, fine. I'll see you then. [Puts phone down] Sorry about that. Where was I?

ADVISER: You were explaining that you felt as though you were going through a dry patch spiritually.

VICAR: Yes, thank you. I've been feeling that somehow

I've just been going through the motions, as though somehow all those things that I believe in aren't quite real, that . . . [Phone rings] Sorry about this. Please excuse me again. Hello. Yes . . . Well I thought that the Women's Group was seeing to that this week . . . Can you phone Mrs Brown and let her know what's happening . . . Yes, I'll be down there about half an hour earlier to sort out the boiler and make sure the heating is on. [Puts phone down] Sorry about that. Problems with the church cleaning rotas. What were you saying?

ADVISER: You must stop and *listen*. Slow down. You're doing too much.

The need to go on listening

Yet a parable will go on yielding insights to us, asking us questions, if we keep opening ourselves to its message. For one more time, let's notice the story of the Good Samaritan (Luke 10.30–37). It is usually taken to mean that we should help someone in need, even when that person is someone we despise (as jews despised samaritans). But if that was what Jesus meant, surely it would have been better to make the wounded man a samaritan and the one who helped him an ordinary jew? What Jesus seems to intend is to challenge his hearers to put together two mutually exclusive words for the same person – 'Samaritan' (verse 33) and 'neighbour' (verse 36). By challenging a jewish audience to think of the same person as both 'Samaritan' and 'neighbour', he is turning upside-down their assumptions about the world, and God's view on it. Rather than simply exhorting people to help others in need, he is inviting them into a new discovery of God's grace, and the person who has discovered that grace can respond with a new freedom to the command, 'You go, then, and do the same' (verse 37).

This persistent listening to a parable, allowing our assumptions to be questioned by it and expecting to receive fresh insights, is probably what Jesus is getting at in his difficult saying about the purpose of parables. To his disciples he said: 'You have been given the secret of the kingdom of God. But the others, who are on the outside, hear all things by means of parables, so that,

> They may look and look,
> yet not see;
> they may listen and listen,
> yet not understand.
> For if they did, they would turn to God,
> and he would forgive them' (Mark 4.11–12).

This *sounds* as though he is deliberately talking in riddles in order to keep the truth from people. But that hardly squares with the general impression we get of Jesus from the gospels. Jesus means that he does not dish out truth in tidy packages to be accepted or rejected with superficial thought. Only when people 'work at' the meaning of the parable and allow themselves to be grasped by it do they really 'see the point' and discover the grace and demand of the kingdom of God. For some people, then as now, Jesus' parables are merely marvellous stories. But for those who commit themselves to *acting* on what the stories say, they open a door into the life which only God can give.

Summary

In this chapter we have noticed how differences between the gospels are due to the writers' concern to add information, to put a particular theological slant on the story, to communicate it in an appropriate way to their readers. Differences do not arise for arbitrary or perverse reasons.

We have observed how each writer has his own special emphases, the insights which make his own portrait of Jesus distinctive.

We have found that interpretation of a passage involves asking the right questions:

What did it mean for the writer and his readers?
- What is its context – historically, culturally, etc.?
- What is its context within the gospel?
- What is its content – words, sentences, paragraphs?

What is its significance for us?
- What principles does the passage express?
- How do they apply in our context?

And we have related these guidelines especially to the study of Jesus' parables.

Questions for discussion

1 'Differences between the gospels do not arise because the writers make arbitrary changes or are unconcerned about truth' (page 35). Is it possible *both* to recognize that there are differences between the gospels *and* to regard the gospels as reliable accounts of Jesus' ministry and message?

2 It is normal practice in church services or in bible study to read and reflect on short sections of a gospel – something we would not do with a novel or a history book. Do you think we lose anything important by studying short sections rather than whole gospels?

3 Study Luke 12.13–21, making use of the questions listed at the end of this chapter.

4 Rewrite this parable in a modern version. (This may be done in pairs. Try not to make your versions much longer than Jesus' parable.)

4

Understanding the letters

Most of the New Testament books are letters, and most of those letters are from Paul. So we shall look especially at Paul's letters, taking 1 Corinthians as an example. Paul's letters are, in fact, the earliest documents in the New Testament, dating from perhaps AD 48 (Galatians) to the end of his life in the mid-sixties of the first century. Incidentally, the order of Paul's letters in our New Testaments bears no relation to the order in which he wrote them. They are arranged in order of length, from the longest to the shortest, except that the letters to individuals – Timothy, Titus and Philemon – are all grouped together at the end.

Why did Paul write letters? For the same reason that most of us write letters: as a substitute for personal presence. I am not in the habit of writing letters to my family, because I see them every day. But if I am away from home for a period, I may write to give news, to express love or concern, perhaps to give advice on something that has cropped up. In a similar way Paul the apostle writes to a church what he would say if he were present. We can see this from hints in some letters. He ends 1 Thessalonians with the instruction: 'I urge you by the authority of the Lord to read this letter to all the believers' (5.27). It's as though his letter represents the kind of sermon he would preach if he were there. The writer of the short letters, 2 and 3 John, says that his letters are simply stop gaps to encourage his readers until a personal visit is possible (see 2 John 12; 3 John 13).

There was no public postal service. Letters had to be carried by personal messengers, such as Phoebe, who delivered the letter to the Romans (Romans 16.1), and Stephanas and friends who presumably took 1 Corinthians back to Corinth (1 Corinthians 16.17).

When we write letters we normally follow certain conventions or 'rules'. We put our address and the date at the top right hand corner. We begin 'Dear . . .' and we end 'Yours sincerely', or 'Love from . . .' Paul, too, follows the familiar practice of his day. Although his letters are usually much longer than a typical first-century letter, they have the same basic shape:

1 *Greeting*. A Greek letter would begin like this: 'From Didymus to Apollinarius, greetings'. So Paul begins, 'From Paul, who was called by the will of God to be an apostle of Christ Jesus, and from our brother Sosthenes, to the church of God which is in Corinth . . . grace and peace' (1 Corinthians 1.1–3). Paul has elaborated the basic pattern to give it a solemn ring and a christian framework. He has altered the conventional 'greetings' (Greek *chairein*) to the similar sounding word for 'grace' (*charis*), and has added the jewish greeting 'peace' (*shalom*). Thus is new life breathed into old phrases.

2 *Thanksgiving*. A Greek letter often included thanks to the gods for good health or a safe journey. Paul offers thanks for the faith of his churches (1 Corinthians 1.4–9). Only in Galatians is he so agitated that he dispenses with thanksgiving and launches straight into his argument!

3 *The main body of the letter*. In a Greek letter this might include personal news and instructions to the recipient. In Paul's letters its contents vary according to the situation of his readers. But typically there is personal information – for example, about his travel plans – and teaching and exhortations to his readers. This may cover a whole

range of necessary themes, as in 1 Corinthians 1.10 to 16.18.

4 *Conclusion*. A Greek letter may wish good health to the recipient and his family. Paul's christian version of this is to wish the grace of the Lord Jesus to be with his readers (1 Corinthians 16.23). Some letters, if not all, were dictated to a secretary, and Paul wrote a personal greeting at the end (see 1 Corinthians 16.21).

So we see how Paul follows the pattern of letter-writing familiar in his own day. But he adapts it to his purposes, and forges something distinctively christian out of the conventions of greeting, thanksgiving and conclusion. The fact that Paul's thought is expressed in letters has some important implications for our understanding.

Letters as conversations

Paul's letters are real letters addressed to real people, discussing real situations and real problems. This means that we must try to understand the situations to which he is responding; but this involves detective work, since we have no one to tell us exactly what was going on in Corinth, or Thessalonica, or wherever Paul's letter was addressed to. We have to work it out as best we can from the letter itself. It's like listening to one end of a telephone conversation. Sometimes it is not too difficult to guess what is being said at the other end of the line. At other times what we hear remains puzzling.

When studying 1 Corinthians, which will be our main example for study in this chapter, we find some issues fairly easy to understand. For instance, Paul begins chapter five with a clear statement of an issue. 'Now, it is actually being said that there is sexual immorality among you so terrible that not even the heathen would be guilty of it. I am told that a man is sleeping with his stepmother!' That may be shocking, but it isn't obscure. We can recognize the problem, and the point of Paul's response to it. And with several other issues in 1 Corinthians, Paul gives away enough information for us to visualize what was going on. But it's a different matter when we come to 1 Corinthians 15.29; 'Now, what about those people who are baptized for the dead?' No one really knows what this means. The practice is not mentioned elsewhere in the New Testament. Paul doesn't say whether he approves of it. Perhaps some christians in Corinth had relatives who had died before they had a chance to be baptized, and so these christians thought they could secure their relatives' salvation by getting baptized on their behalf. But that is only a guess. Paul refers to the practice – without saying whether he approves or disapproves – in order to say that their denial of belief in the resurrection of christians is inconsistent with their practice of baptism on behalf of the dead. For he goes on, 'If it is true, as some claim, that the dead are not raised to life, why are those people being baptized for the dead?'

The precise meaning of this practice is not very important for us because we can get the drift of that argument against those who deny the resurrection. A much greater problem is raised by 2 Thessalonians 2, where Paul is teaching about the climax of history and the final coming of Christ. Having mentioned 'the final Rebellion' and the appearance of 'the Wicked One' (verse 3), he continues: 'Don't you remember? I told you all this while I was with you. Yet there is something that keeps it from happening now, and you know what it is' (verses 5–6). Well, Paul's readers may have known, but we have hardly a clue. In a case like this, where the gap in our understanding is obvious because we only have one end of the conversation, we are wise to admit ignorance. Certainly, it would be foolish to build a doctrine on such tantalizingly incomplete information.

Another implication of Paul's letters being addressed to real and specific situations is that they don't give carefully balanced, systematic teaching. We have from him detailed discussions of the Lord's Supper and of worship in general (1 Corinthians 11–14), only because these matters were causing upheavals among the Corinthian christians. The Lord's Supper is not mentioned elsewhere by Paul, or in any other New Testament letter. And because some of Paul's letters were written in the heat of controversy, he can appear to be saying contradictory things in different letters. In Galatians, for example, he proclaims, 'Freedom is what we have – Christ has set us free! Stand, then, as free people, and do not allow yourselves to become slaves again' (Galatians 5.1). In contrast to this insistence on freedom from the law of Moses, in 1 Corinthians Paul tries to put reins in the 'christian liberty' of his readers. The emphasis has to be different because the situation is different. In Galatians Paul is arguing with teachers who insist that gentiles must submit to the jewish law if they wish to belong to the people of God. In 1 Corinthians he is confronted by people who claim that Christ has set them free from all kinds of moral restraint.

So we don't have the whole of Paul's thought. We only have his response to those situations in his churches which provoked letters from him. And we don't even have all his letters. He himself mentions at least one which doesn't survive, when he mentions 'the letter that I wrote to you' in 1 Corinthians 5.9. Yet, if I had the choice between letters such as Paul's and systematic statements of theology, I would choose letters every time! For they bring us close to the realities of life for those first christians. They are forged in controversy, bursting with vitality. They are about Christianity in practice, not in theory. They are the outpourings of the heart of a missionary whose faith has been refined by persecution.

Read 2 Corinthians 6.3–10 and 11.23 to 12.10 for a glimpse into what Paul went through, and how the power of God was at work through it all.

Different kinds of letters

If we widen our horizons to include the other letters of the New Testament, we notice that there are three or four different kinds of letters. We have seen that Paul's letters to churches are based on the normal letter-writing patterns of the day. They are written to real people in specific situations. Under Paul's name there are also letters to individuals – 1 and 2 Timothy, Titus, and Philemon. These follow a similar pattern, though 1 Timothy and Titus don't have a thanksgiving section. But there are other letters – James and 1 and 2 Peter – which are written as letters but are addressed to a wide audience in various destinations. James begins grandly: 'Greetings to all God's people scattered over the whole world'! Letters like this obviously don't address specific situations, though they no doubt reflect the prevailing conditions under which most of their readers lived. They are a bit like the letter which an archbishop might send to the churches in his country, commenting in a general way about issues confronting the Church.

In some ways, perhaps, the general nature of such letters makes them easier to apply to ourselves. We are not looking for very specific backgrounds against which to interpret them, as is the case with Paul's letters. So, for example, we find echoes in our own experience when we read what James says about trials of our faith (1.2–4, 12–15), difficulties in prayer (1.6–8), the peril of hearing God's word without obeying it (1.22–27; 2.14–26), the power of the tongue for good or evil (3.1–12), the dangers of wealth (5.1–6).

One other group of letters consists of those which *are* addressed to specific churches, but don't look much like letters. Most of Hebrews looks more like an elaborate sermon than a letter. Its author isn't named. But the reference to its readers' previous experience of suffering (10.32–34) shows that it is addressed to a particular group of people. And suddenly, at the end, the normal features of a letter appear: the writer asks for prayer 'that God will send me back to you soon' (13.22–25). The First Letter of John has none of the normal features of a letter, but it is written to a group whom the author knows intimately. 'My children', he keeps calling them. When studying any of these letters which have a specific audience in mind, it is important for us to learn what we can about their situation in order to appreciate the aims and impact of the letter.

Guidelines for interpretation

It's time we summarized some guidelines for interpreting the New Testament letters. As we saw with the gospels, it's a matter of asking the right questions. First, we ask about what a letter originally *meant*.

1 *What impression do we get from the letter as a whole?* If we receive a lengthy letter from a friend or from our bank manager, we read it as a whole. We would think it odd to read a paragraph without reference to the rest of the letter. Often a paragraph which looks puzzling or alarming makes sense in the context of the whole letter. So it is with New Testament letters. And it is easier to see the shape of the whole than it is with a gospel. Even a long letter like 1 Corinthians is little more than half the length of Mark's gospel.

A read through 1 Corinthians would yield the following observations about the letter's aims and themes. Paul is in Ephesus (1 Corinthians 16.8) and has got news from two sources of problems arising at Corinth. 'Some people from Chloe's family' (1.11) – probably slaves of a wealthy Corinthian woman – have come to Paul with news of divisive factions in the Corinthian Church (1.10 to 4.21). They have also reported immorality (chapter 5; 6.12–20), legal disputes between christians (6.1–11) and abuse of the Lord's Supper (11.17–34). Paul has also received a letter from the Corinthian church about matters where there is disagreement among them. He deals one by one with the issues they raise. 'Now, to deal with the matters you wrote about,' he begins (7.1), and launches into questions about marriage (chapter 7). Other matters are introduced with the phrase, 'Now, concerning what you wrote about . . .' (7.25; 8.1; 12.1; 16.1). We may list these, together with two other matters which are not specifically introduced by a reference to the Corinthians' letter: the problem of meat offered to idols (8.1 to 11.1), a problem about covering one's head in worship (11.2–16), spiritual gifts (chapters 12–14), belief in the resurrection (chapter 15), the collection for impoverished christians in Judea (16.1–4).

Awareness of this general shape of the letter will give us confidence to find our way around it. It will give us insight into how Paul feels about the Corinthian Church and *why* he is so exasperated with them. It will help us to see *connections* between the different problems which crop up. They are not just a rag-bag of pastoral nightmares, but different manifestations of the tendency of some Corinthian christians to be divisive, arrogant, lacking in love. Notice how, in the light of these tendencies, Paul argues several times that the cross of Christ is the sole basis of christian living and cuts human arrogance down to size (1.17 to 2.5; 5.7–8; 11.17–34). And love is the only proper response to Christ (8.1; 13.1 to 14.1; 16.14). Now we have some general idea of the letter's message, we shall make more sense of shorter passages.

2 *What is the context?* This breaks down into two parts. First, what is the letter's context in terms of history and geography, and the world of thought of the writer and his readers? In the case of 1 Corinthians, for example, geography plays a role. Look at a map and you can see what a strategic place it holds. Not only does it command the narrow strip of land joining northern and southern Greece, it also controlled seaports facing both east and west. Rather than sail all the way round the stormy coast of southern Greece, many ships' captains preferred to have their vessels lifted out of the sea at Corinth and hauled on rollers along a trackway which connected Corinth's western and eastern ports. This strategic position of course made Corinth wealthy, and it made the Corinthian population very cosmopolitan, always open to new ideas. This made it easy at first for Paul to get a hearing, but it also meant that, once he had formed a church, he had constantly to battle with conflicting and dangerous ideas.

Let me also illustrate one way in which awareness of Paul's and his readers' world of thought helps our understanding. If I mention some of the terms Paul uses to refer to salvation, to many people they will sound daunting and 'academic'. Justification, redemption, reconciliation, sacrifice – these sound like the heavy technical terms of the theologian looking for ways to make things complicated. But, in fact, for Paul and his readers they are not technical terms, loaded with centuries of subtle debate. They are vivid metaphors. Paul's readers know what it is to be taken to the law court and to be declared 'in the right' – justified ('put right', *GNB* 1 Corinthians 6.11). In a world where slaves are constantly bought and sold, and sometimes set free, they know what it is to be 'bought for a price' – redeemed (1 Corinthians 6.20). They know about city states making peace with each other after a period of hostility – being reconciled ('changing enemies into friends', *GNB* 2 Corinthians 5.18, 20). They are familiar with sacrifice as a means of restoring relations between man and God. So when they hear that through Christ and his sacrifice they are justified, redeemed, reconciled to God, they are being gripped by vivid metaphors. Rather than dismissing such terms as unnecessary technical jargon, we must try to appreciate the power of such images.

The second question we must ask about context is, What is the context of the passage within the letter? Let's take two examples from 1 Corinthians. In 2.2 Paul writes, 'While I was with you, I made up my mind to forget everything except Jesus Christ and especially his death on the cross'. It has often been suggested that Paul is here reporting how, after the 'failure' of his attempt to mix the gospel with Greek philosophy at Athens (Acts 17), he came to Corinth (Acts 18) with different tactics, determined to preach only the cross. There is in fact no evidence for this view. The author of Acts didn't see himself as describing a failure due to wrong tactics by his hero in Athens. And if we look at Paul's words in their context in 1 Corinthians, we can see that he is *not* contrasting his method at Corinth with his method at Athens. He is contrasting his own way of preaching with the arrogant and clever talk of some influential preachers in Corinth. Notice what he says about 'boasting' in 1.29–31, and link this with what we have observed already about the arrogance of some Corinthians.

Few who listen with starry eyes to the reading of 1 Corinthians 13 at a wedding are aware of the real context of Paul's 'hymn to love'. The context is not marriage, but the controversy over spiritual gifts, especially speaking in tongues. The love which Paul describes is the framework of relationships within which gifts are to be used. Without it, the most exciting and stupendous gift is worth absolutely nothing. Now I am not saying that 1 Corinthians 13 is an inappropriate reading for a wedding. Many scholars think that Paul had written this passage on some other occasion and included it here, ready-made, because it fitted his argument about spiritual gifts. So maybe Paul himself used it in other more general contexts. Nevertheless, the only place where it is available to us is sandwiched between chapters twelve and fourteen, and so our first responsibility is to understand its point in that context. Incidentally, the presence of chapter thirteen here is an important argument against those who argue that the gifts discussed in chapters twelve and fourteen should not be welcomed in the Church today. There is no good reason for saying that chapter thirteen is a message for today, whilst chapters twelve and fourteen are not. 1 Corinthians 13.10 itself says that the gifts will disappear only 'when what is perfect comes', and that means when we share in God's eternal, perfect kingdom when 'we shall see face to face' (verse 12).

3 *What is the content of the passage?* We take as an example 1 Corinthians 8–10, where Paul deals with a disagreement about meat which has been sacrificed to idols. To us this may sound an obscure and irrelevant problem, but we must explore what the issue actually was. A careful study of the passage – with perhaps a bit of help from a commentary or bible dictionary – will reveal that Paul has been asked for guidance on a threefold problem. Can christians buy meat in the market, even though it may be surplus from sacrifices at nearby pagan temples (10.25)? Can they accept an invitation to dinner in the local temple dining room, even though the meal will begin and end with a sacrifice to the god (8.10; 10.14–22)? Can they accept an invitation to dinner at a friend's home, where

the meat *may* have come via the market from a pagan temple sacrifice (10.27)? The questions are complicated by the fact that conflicting viewpoints have been argued by christians in Corinth. Some, who think of themselves as liberated, see no problem with any of these cases. Since 'idols' – the Greek gods worshipped at the temples – don't actually exist, then it can do no harm to eat sacrificed meat or even to attend a temple ceremony. Others, however, are troubled. As recent converts from paganism, they have tender consciences, and if they see other christians cheerfully eating the sacrificed meat they fear they may be lured back into the grip of paganism (8.7, 10).

In response, Paul first agrees in principle with the 'liberated' ones who argue that, since idols don't exist, there is no reason for rejecting the meat (8.4–6): you can buy it in the market (10.25–26). But then he argues that one's 'freedom' or 'rights' are less important than the unity of the christian fellowship, and care for one's christian brother. Love is more important than knowledge (8.1–3 – 'knowledge' here implies that attitude of arrogant superiority which we noticed earlier). If my eating meat at a temple dinner tempts a recent convert from idol-worship to slip back into his old ways, I am ruining a brother for whom Christ died. So christian love requires that, for my brother's sake, I refrain from using my freedom (8.7–13). The truly liberated person is not one who insists on his freedom in all circumstances, but one who can forgo his freedom for the sake of others. And this is where chapter nine comes in. It is not a digression about Paul's apostleship; it is there as a personal example of forgoing one's rights for the sake of others. Paul is saying, 'In urging you to limit your freedom, I am not asking you to do anything which I haven't been willing to do myself. As an apostle I have certain rights, but I have gone without them for the sake of my mission, for the sake of others.'

But there is a further limitation which Paul insists on. Participation in sacrificial ceremonies at Greek temples is forbidden because it exposes people to demonic forces which blind them to God's truth. It is incompatible with participation in the Lord's Supper (10.1–22, especially verses 18–22). There is room for flexibility, however, when christians are invited to eat in the home of non-christian friends. Because there is nothing evil about the meat itself, they may eat what is put before them without raising any questions. But if someone (presumably another guest, with a 'weak' conscience) informs them that the meat has indeed been sacrificed in the temple, they should refrain from eating it, for the sake of the weaker christian (10.27–29).

So Paul has dealt with a matter of dispute, partly by declaring what is *not* permitted for any christian – involvement in worship of other 'gods'; and saying *why* – it exposes one to demonic powers. And where differing opinions are acceptable, he gives guidelines for deciding one's course of action: love means that I will not act so as to cause my brother to stumble. All this can be gained from a careful reading of the content of Paul's chapters. But then we must go on to our next question.

4. *What is the passage's significance for us?* Surprisingly, perhaps, for such a passage, there is a quite direct application for some christians. Imagine yourself, as part of a plan to develop good relations in the local community, going with a group to meet local hindus at their temple. As part of their hospitality towards you, they will offer you *prasada*, sweet food which has been dedicated at worship in the temple. Do you accept it, thinking that it would be rude to refuse? Or do you refuse, because it is 'food offered to idols'? Would acceptance mean laying yourself open to demonic influence? Of course, there are big issues here which we can't go into now, about the

nature of non-christian religions and God's view of their adherents. But Paul's argument suggests that it is appropriate to eat the food offered as long as it does not involve you in *worship* of gods other than 'the God and Father of our Lord Jesus Christ'. But if one of your group is a new christian who was until recently a hindu, and still feels the pull of his former way of worship, then your desire not to put a stumbling-block in his way will mean that you refuse the food. Incidentally, it is perfectly possible to do this without showing disrespect for your hosts, just as it would be possible for a hindu visiting my home to refuse meat without showing disrespect for me.

However, even when 1 Corinthians 8–10 cannot be applied to quite such a comparable situation as this, there are *principles* in Paul's argument which are significant for many situations. A list of such principles might include the following:

Love is more important than knowledge.

Material things are not evil in themselves, but may have evil consequences arising from the context in which they are used.

Freedom of action must not be insisted on if it would cause a weaker christian to stumble.

Exposure to demonic activity is not an option for the christian.

It is not enough to ask whether a course of action is permitted; we should ask whether it is good and helpful, and whether it will bring glory to God.

Once we are aware of such principles, we must be careful to apply them in genuinely *comparable* situations. That is, they apply where christian consciences differ, and where for the 'liberated' christian to insist on his freedom could cause another's faith to falter. This is *not* the same as a situation where one christian's action may *offend* another. I suspect that christians may quite often be called to do something which offends some other christian, just as Jesus' mixing with the outcast often offended his religious contemporaries. The question is, could my action, though permissible in itself, be a stumbling-block to another christian for whom following my example would create problems? This question might arise over our use of Sunday. Or it would affect our thinking about what to drink at a celebration meal if there were an ex-alcoholic in the group.

A striking example is reported by Paul Little in his book *How to Give Away Your Faith*. He met a salesman who had literally worshipped baseball before he became a christian. When he overheard Paul Little suggesting to a friend that they go to watch a baseball match, he stared incredulously and demanded, 'How can you as a christian go to a baseball game?' Little's initial amazement gradually turned into understanding of the man's problem. Because baseball had been such a big thing for him – an idol – he assumed that anyone who watched baseball was worshipping it as an idol. So the baseball date was cancelled because to have gone would have needlessly disturbed the salesman at a sensitive stage of his christian life.

There are two further points which are implied in Paul's treatment of this issue. First, he doesn't expect that those of 'weak conscience' will always remain weak. He expects them to mature, so that what is a problem for them now may not always be so. Thus a christian's sensitivity to his brother will not always call for the same response in every situation. Paul Little's salesman came to recognize that he shouldn't legislate for christians who have no problem with baseball. The second point is that christians must go on listening to each other over matters on which they disagree. Unity can emerge only from discussion, not from entrenched positions.

Summary

In this chapter we have seen that New Testament letters were written as a substitute for what the writer would say if he were present with his readers. All, except the letters of James, Peter and Jude, were addressed to quite specific situations. As a result of this, letters do not give systematic teaching but apply the gospel to particular issues. Sometimes those issues are hard for us to understand because we have access only to one end of the conversation. Interpretation of the letters involves asking:

What impression do we get from the letter as a whole?
What is the context of a passage?
What is its content?
What is its significance for us?

We have seen how asking these questions involves us in discovering what the letter says to its readers' situation and why it says it, in order to draw out principles which we can apply to comparable situations today.

Questions for discussion

1 What, in your experience, are the joys and difficulties of reading New Testament letters? In what ways has the reading of this chapter helped you to come to terms with the difficulties?

2 Some families in your church are planning a Hallowe'en party to which children are asked to come dressed as witches. But other parents, concerned about the fascination of the occult, won't let their children attend and think the party should be cancelled. How would you try to resolve the disagreement in the light of the principles which Paul gives in 1 Corinthians 8–10? (Try to ensure that you *are* applying Paul's principles, rather than just

talking generally about the issue. You may prefer to discuss some other issue over which christians disagree.)

3 How can we ensure that our reading of the New Testament leads to action as well as reflection?

4 Study Philippians 1.12–26, or 1 Thessalonians 5.1–11, or Hebrews 12.1–11, or 1 Peter 1.1–9. Using the questions listed at the end of this chapter, try to discover the thrust of what the author was saying to his original readers, and then what the passage's significance may be for your group. (The group leader may need to summarize the general aims and context of the letter, making use of the introduction to the letter in the *Good News Bible*, and perhaps a commentary too. It will be necessary to devise more specific questions to enable your group to discover the meaning of your chosen passage and its significance for your group.)

5

One faith in many forms

This chapter is a bit of a rag-bag. We shall dip into the two types of New Testament literature which haven't been mentioned so far: the Acts of the Apostles and the Revelation to John. And we shall reflect on the varieties of faith which are expressed in these and other New Testament books.

Acts – Luke's second volume

Acts is the only book of its kind in the New Testament, the only narrative of the early Church's life. Yet of course, being a narrative, it has much in common with the gospels. It is, in fact, the second volume of Luke's two-volume work, and it is a pity that this fact is obscured by John's gospel being sandwiched between them in the New Testament. We can see the link with Luke's gospel from the way Acts begins: 'Dear Theophilus: In my first book I wrote about all the things that Jesus did and taught . . .' (Acts 1.1).

But what kind of a book is it? Why should anyone hit on the idea of charting the story of the first christians? And if it is a history of the early church, why is it so vague about dates? Why is it nearly all about Peter and Paul, and very little about other apostles? Why does it say nothing about the church in Galilee (apart from the summary in 9.31)? Why does it end at such an odd point, with Paul under house-arrest in Rome?

We could go on asking questions. And we should! We may not always find the answers, but it's by asking questions like these that we learn to sniff out what a book is driving at. If we ask, for example, why it is written like this – rather than in the way we might have expected it to be written – we are half way to discovering what the author really wants to tell us.

Before thinking about what God, through Luke, wants to say to us in this book, we must notice what he may *not* want to say. It is commonly assumed among christians that narrative books, such as Acts, are there to provide the church with examples to follow. They read Acts looking for a pattern which they can copy in their own lives or the corporate life of the Church. The first christians in Jerusalem 'would sell their property and possessions, and distribute the money among all' (2.45). So we must do the same. The people in Samaria who were converted through Philip's preaching did not 'receive the Holy Spirit' until Peter and John rolled up from Jerusalem and laid hands on them (8.14–17). So we must expect reception of the Spirit as an experience given through the laying on of hands at a time later than conversion. So the Pentecostalists say. Or we must insist on the need for confirmation by bishops (who are successors of the apostles) through the laying on of hands. So those of a more Catholic viewpoint say. In either case they are giving to a narrative description the role of a normative guide. They are turning a description into a prescription.

Now I am not saying that a narrative in Acts never provides us with an example to follow. Sometimes, for instance, God may use the statement that some christians sold their property to challenge a modern-day christian to take a similar radical and costly step with his own property. Yet it is wrong to turn a description into a prescription for everyone. The fact that John the Baptist ate locusts, or that Jesus rode a donkey, does not mean that we should do the same. The fact that Paul proceeded on his final journey to Jerusalem, despite having been warned by the prophet Agabus that he would be arrested there (21.10–14), does not mean that we should always run knowingly into danger.

We can only be confident that a narrative description offers an example to follow if it is clear that the writer *intended* it as such. I shall show some instances of this in Acts later. Meanwhile, I repeat that description does not necessarily mean prescription. And the opposite of this is equally important: the fact that a particular practice is *not* described in the New Testament does not of itself mean that the practice is wrong for christians. I have met people who thought that we shouldn't use hymn-books because they aren't mentioned in the New Testament, or argued that we shouldn't use microphones to preach the gospel because Paul didn't. They have fallen into this trap of deciding what is appropriate according to whether it is described in the New Testament. Questions about hymn-books and microphones, and a host of other things, have to be decided in the light of whether they are consistent with the general intentions of the New Testament or with general principles which can be drawn from it.

The shape of Acts

If we are to get some overall sense of what Luke means us to learn from Acts, we need to read it right through. As I suggested in our discussion of the gospels, it is a good idea to read the whole book at one or two sittings, noting any points to which Luke appears to give special attention. The following discussion aims to pick out some of them.

Luke offers a clue to his intentions in the five summary statements which occur at Acts 6.7; 9.31; 12.24; 16.5; 19.20. The first one, for instance, says: 'And so the word of God continued to spread. The number of disciples in Jerusalem grew larger and larger, and a great number of priests accepted the faith.' At each point Luke is pausing to sum up 'the story so far', before moving on to a new stage of the narrative. Thus Acts is divided into six sections, each covering a different stage in the church's progress. 1.1 to 6.7 portrays the earliest church in Jerusalem. 6.8 to 9.31 covers the church growth into Samaria through the witness of Greek-speaking jews such as Stephen. It also includes the conversion of Paul, who is to become prominent at a later stage. 9.32 to 12.24 describes the first outreach to gentiles, in the shape of Cornelius and later the people of Antioch.

Throughout those three sections Peter is the dominant figure. For the rest of Acts Paul takes centre-stage. 12.25 to 16.5 shows him taking the gospel outside Palestine–Syria into the gentile world of Cyprus and Asia Minor (Turkey). 16.6 to 19.20 describes further expansion into Europe, and 19.21 to 28.31 sees Paul finally reaching Rome.

This scheme seems to have some connection with Acts 1.8, where the risen Jesus says to the apostles, 'When the Holy Spirit comes upon you, you will be filled with power, and you will be witnesses for me in Jerusalem, in all Judaea and Samaria and to the ends of the earth'. Both that promise of Christ and the overall shape of Acts suggest that Luke's main interest is in the missionary expansion of the Church. Yet he never actually tells us about witness at 'the ends of the earth'. Rome is hardly that! He doesn't tell us about other apostles and preachers going in other directions. His focus is on the movement from Jerusalem, where Peter is the chief actor, to Rome, where Paul is central. Luke mentions only incidentally (28.15) that the Church was already well established in Rome by the time Paul arrived. His presentation of the story reaches its climax with Paul preaching to gentiles in Rome, 'speaking with all boldness and freedom' (28.31). That last phrase of the whole book is clearly meant to express the triumph of God's purpose in bringing the good news to the heart of the empire.

All this suggests that the purpose of Acts is not to record the history of the early Church. It is too selective for that. Luke does give us a historical account, and its accuracy can be confirmed at various points. But it is a narrative designed to convey a message. It is a message about the mission of the church of Christ, which might be summarized under four headings.

First, the story of the church's mission is the story of the gospel increasingly being rejected by jews and accepted by gentiles. Just as Jesus himself saw jews resent his presence and spoke of salvation for gentiles (Luke 4.16–30), so there recurs in Acts the refrain that, because jews reject God's word, the message is being taken to gentiles (13.46; 18.6; 28.25–28). This turning to the gentiles was approved by Palestinian christians such as Peter, who himself preached to Cornelius (Acts 10), and by the Jerusalem church at the council of Jerusalem in Acts 15.

Secondly – and this can hardly be overstressed – the mission is directed and empowered by God himself through his Spirit. At every turn we are shown that God is in control. It was 'the Lord' who daily 'added to their group those who were being saved' (2.47). Persecution in Jerusalem only caused the mission to advance into Samaria (8.4). When the time came for the gentile Cornelius to become a christian, God prepared him through a vision, prepared Peter through a vision to speak to him, and then surprised even Peter by sending the Holy Spirit on Cornelius and his friends while Peter's sermon was still in progress (Acts 10). And just in case anyone didn't get the message about how significant all this was, the whole story is repeated in chapter eleven!

When Paul was travelling through Asia Minor he tried to preach in various places, but the Holy Spirit prevented him (we aren't told how) and pushed him on until he reached the coast at Troas and found himself en route for Europe (16.6–10). It has even been suggested that the point of the long account of Paul's voyage to Rome, shipwreck and rescue (chapter 27) lies in Luke's desire to underline God's control of events. God has promised that Paul will bear witness to Christ before gentiles and rulers (9.15) and in Rome itself (23.11). So despite all obstacles God will ensure that he does just that!

Thirdly, the life and mission of the church mirrors the mission of Jesus. Look again at Acts 1.1, which could well be translated: 'In my first book I wrote about all the things that Jesus *began* to do and to teach . . .' And the implication of this is that what Jesus began during his earthly ministry he is continuing to do through the Holy Spirit in the church. Hence Luke shows us that just as the earthly Jesus had a special concern for the poor, for outcasts, for samaritans and gentiles, so does the church (Acts 4.34–35; 9.36; 11.29; 3.1–10; 8.26–40; 8.4–25; 10, 11; Paul's mission to gentiles). Just as prayer and praise figured prominently in Jesus' life, so they are important for the church (Acts 2.42, 46–47; 4.23–31; 16.25). Just as Jesus was empowered by the Holy Spirit, so is the church (Luke 3.22; 4.1, 14, 18; Acts 1.8; 2.1–4; 38–39).

Fourthly, people are brought to faith through the preaching of God's word. In Acts, Luke devotes a lot of space to summaries of the gospel preached by Peter and Paul (e.g., 2.14–40; 3.12–26; 10.34–43; 13.16–41; 17.22–31; 22.1–21; 26.2–23). If you study these sermons you will see that there is a common core of material running through them, focusing especially on Jesus' death and resurrection. But the emphasis varies according to the type of audience being addressed. The fact that Luke allocates so much space to these speeches surely means that he wants to impress on his readers how the gospel was preached by the Church's first great leaders – so that they in turn will understand what the gospel is for their own contemporaries.

Interpreting Acts

When we come, then, to a passage in Acts, we have to ask our now familiar questions. What is its historical and cultural context? What is its context in the overall plan of Acts? What is its content – what does it say and why? What is its significance for us?

All these questions must be viewed in the light of the author's *intention*, which we have tried to uncover in the last two or three pages. Once we have got a feel for what Luke is intending to emphasize for us, we have a firmer basis for handling those questions with which we began the chapter, about how far narrative passages can serve as *examples* for us.

To discover a passage's significance for us, we cannot simply take it as an example, without paying attention to Luke's wider purpose and message. The practice of selling possessions and giving the proceeds to the poor in Jerusalem (2.45; 4.34–35) is an example which some christian groups today *may* decide to follow. But we cannot say that all christians *must* follow it because Luke does not present it as a *normative* pattern for christians everywhere. The fact that Cornelius spoke in strange tongues when the Holy Spirit came on him (10.46) shows that this *may* happen to others. But it cannot mean that only those with such an experience have genuinely received the Spirit, since Luke records other instances of reception of the Spirit without mentioning the gift of tongues (e.g., Paul in Acts 9.17–19). Indeed, the message which Luke seems to be conveying through his varied accounts of how people first encountered the Holy Spirit is that God is sovereign in the giving of the Spirit. He does his work in his own way, acts differently with different people, and cannot be tied down to a ritual or a formula.

However, over some issues it is the *intention* of Acts to provide examples. Luke wants us to learn what the essential gospel is, and to see that it must be expressed in different ways for different audiences. He wants us to learn to trust in the direction and enabling power of God in mission. He wants us to follow Jesus' example in concern for the least, the last, and the lost. He wants the church to be characterized by mission, by prayer and by experience of the Spirit. We are right to look in Acts for examples to follow as long as they are consistent with these key themes – or with other themes which we find Luke emphasizing throughout his book.

Thus when we study the story of Paul and Silas and the gaoler in Philippi (16.22–40) we should not see it as instruction on what to do during earthquakes or how to deal with potential suicides, since those factors are peculiar to this episode. But the story does show how God is in control even when his servants are imprisoned. It does illustrate the essential gospel and how a person's life is changed through faith in Jesus. And it forcibly demonstrates that Paul's innocence was acknowledged by Roman officials. This is another recurring theme in Acts (18.12–17; 19.35–41; 25.25; 26.32; compare Luke 23.13–16, on the innocence of Jesus). It seems to be one of Luke's purposes to demonstrate that christians have never been found guilty of rebellion against the state or of creating public disorder – and therefore the church and the state should have nothing to fear from each other.

A final example is the account of Paul's famous disagreement with Barnabas in Acts 15.36–41. When Paul proposed to Barnabas that they re-visit churches founded during their first missionary journey, Barnabas wanted to take Mark with them. But Paul refused, because Mark had backed out of the previous mission when the going got tough. So Barnabas (with Mark) and Paul (with Silas) went off in different directions. Now what is Luke's point in this passage? He gives no hint that he is moralizing about disagreements among christians, or that he is commending Barnabas for giving Mark a second chance. Sermons about how Mark developed after being given this second chance, so that Paul himself came to value him, are better based on Colossians 4.10 and 2 Timothy 4.11 than on this passage.

If we can discern a point in this passage, it may be that, despite disagreements among his servants, God can move his purpose forward. Because of the split, there are now two missions going on, not one! Or perhaps the passage is no more than a transition to the next stage, showing how Paul came to be the leader of the mission to gentiles. That may not be a very exciting lesson to gain from a paragraph in Acts. But we must recognize that often the purpose of a narrative lies not in a single paragraph but in the unfolding drama of a whole book or a whole series of paragraphs. In just the same way, the point of the story of David and Bathsheba in 2 Samuel 11–12, is not primarily to teach that adultery is a bad thing. It is part of the much bigger story of how God's purposes for his people are worked out through – and in spite of – the leadership of David.

The Revelation to John

The last book of the Bible is the most baffling. Many people have capitalized on its ambiguities in order to produce detailed schemes of the progress of world history towards its end. Many others have abandoned it in frustration, or have simply left it unread, assuming that there was nothing in it for them. D. H. Lawrence wrote that, just as Jesus inevitably had to have a Judas among his disciples, so there had to be a Revelation in the New Testament!

Even more than with other books, it is essential for us to grasp what *kind* of a book Revelation is, if we are to make headway with it. We cannot read it the same way as we read Acts, any more than we read Tolkien's *Lord of the Rings* as though it were Churchill's *History of the English-Speaking Peoples*. As usual, we find that the author himself gives clues about the nature of his book.

He says that it is a *revelation* (1.1), a God-given insight into 'what must happen very soon'. That word, 'revelation', translates the Greek *apokalypsis*, from which we get our words 'apocalypse' and 'apocalyptic'. Now, by using this word as his title, John is telling us that his book belongs to the group of writings known as 'apocalyptic literature'. To be sure, this is the only apocalyptic book in the Bible – though parts of Isaiah, Ezekiel, Zechariah and Daniel, and a few New Testament passages such as Mark 13, have a similar 'tone'. But numerous apocalyptic books were produced by jews and christians between 200 BC and AD 200. Apocalyptic is the kind of literature written when times are bad. It is produced by people on the under-side of society. Their experience of oppression by hostile rulers leads them to pin their faith, not so much on God bringing deliverance *within* history, as on God bringing history to an *end*, and replacing it with his kingdom of justice and peace.

Knowing that the Revelation to John follows in this well-worn tradition helps us in understanding it. Jewish apocalypses often divide history into periods and enjoy the use of numbers, giving symbolic significance to numbers such as seven and ten. But their main purpose was not to give precise timetables of future events. By their carefully schematized description of events, they were declaring their faith that, despite all appearances to the contrary, God's purpose would ultimately win through, and his faithful people would be delivered. This should warn us against assuming that Revelation itself intends to give detailed predictions.

Apocalyptic literature is fond of symbols. Symbolism is a language that has to be learnt. A symbol familiar in one culture is unfamiliar, or means something different, in another. In Chinese tradition the dragon is a benevolent creature, but in my culture it often represents evil powers, and certainly does so for John. Although the weird symbolism of his book is difficult for us, it would convey meaning to his readers just as we quite easily recognize the symbolism of a lion, a bear or an eagle in a political cartoon.

As well as being apocalypse, John's book is *prophecy* (1.3). Like Old Testament prophets, John speaks God's word to particular situations, and expresses God's warnings of judgement and promises of deliverance. The letters to the seven churches in chapters two and three look very like some Old Testament prophetic statements, with their warnings and encouragements. The rest of the book draws heavily on passages from Old Testament prophets and re-moulds them for a new situation.

But Revelation is also a *letter*. In 1.4 John uses the normal letter greeting which we discussed in our study of the letters. Not merely the 'letters to the seven churches' in chapters two and three, but the whole book is addressed to particular people known to the author. He knows their circumstances, and expects them to understand what he writes. If you look at a map (*GNB* p. 184), see how a messenger would have carried round the document to the seven churches in the order given in 1.11. Most scholars believe that John was writing to them during the reign of the emperor Domitian (AD 81–96).

He issued a decree demanding to be called 'Lord and God'. Christians, whose loyalty to Christ made them unable to submit to this demand, saw the clouds of persecution and martyrdom gathering. Revelation is a letter to them, from one who himself suffers exile on the island of Patmos because of his witness to Christ (1.9). Who is this John? We don't know, but it is unlikely that he was John the apostle, or he would surely have identified himself as such.

The message of Revelation

What kind of message would christians need in that context? As persecution threatened, they were asking, 'Where is God in all this? Who is in control? Does power lie in the hands of God, or of Domitian?' John's answer is to show them a Christ who was himself 'a faithful witness' in face of suffering, and is now 'the ruler of the kings of the world' (1.5). To people filled with fear this Christ declares, 'Don't be afraid! I am the first and the last. I am the living One! I was dead, but now I am alive for ever and ever. I have authority over death and the world of the dead' (1.17–18). This Lord, who has battled with the forces of evil in his death as the Lamb of God, will see his purpose through to completion. He will bring evil to its end and welcome his people into the 'new heaven and new earth' which is God's destiny for them.

But how do we cope with the mysteries of Revelation? The first step must be to have some sense of the structure of the book, which looks like this:

1.1–8 Prologue.
1.9–20 Vision of the Christ who reveals and rules.
2–3 Prophetic messages to the seven churches.
4–5 Vision of heaven, introducing the main body of the book. God reigns (chapter 4). God's

purposes for present and future can only be understood by looking to the past, to the death and resurrection of Jesus (chapter 5).

6–19 God's judgements on the earth, described in three groups of seven, symbolized as seven seals (chapter 6; 8.1), seven trumpets (chapters 8–9; 11.15–18), seven bowls (chapters 15–16).

Interspersed through this central part of the book are three interludes, which aim chiefly to tell us what happens to the church and what her task is while distress rages around her:

7.1–17 The church is indestructible.

10.1–11.14 The church's task is witness in face of suffering.

12–14 Here conflict between the church and the Roman state is set against the background of the age-long conflict between the powers of darkness and God, between the dragon and the Lamb.

Then comes the climax, the 'tale of two cities' – Babylon (meaning Rome) and the city of God:

17.1–19.10 The fall of Babylon – Rome's anti-christian empire falls prey to its own forces of destruction.

19.11–21 The final coming of Christ.

20.1–15 Christ's thousand year rule and the final judgement.

21–22 The new heaven and new earth.

In a short space we can't hope to unravel the details in all this. But it is the total picture rather than the details which matter in a book like this. Think of it like this. I could play on my piano a G sharp, a C sharp and an E. You would hear the sounds. But it wouldn't be *music* unless I played them in sequence at the appropriate speed and continued with other notes after them. Then you would recognize the pattern of Beethoven's Moonlight Sonata unfolding. Music is a whole sequence of notes, making patterns, creating atmosphere. Break it down into individual notes and you've lost it. It's the same with the vast visions of Revelation. Don't get bogged down in individual bits. Feel the force of whole sections at a time. See how John encourages his readers and strengthens them for the test of suffering. Reflect on what that means for the church today. What *comfort* does it offer to christians under pressure? What *warnings* does it give to a godless world? What does it say about the *task* of the church in face of conflict? How does our *ultimate* hope of eternal life influence our attitude to life now?

God's truth is many-sided

It would be hard to find in the New Testament two books more different from each other than Acts and Revelation. One is narrative, the other is apocalyptic vision. One holds out the hope of a stable and constructive relationship between church and state, the other sees the state as the destructive beast, one day to be laid low by the judgement of God. One is about the expansion of the church, the other is about the church's struggle to survive. Yet, despite the differences, they share the same vital truth: the man Jesus who died on the cross is exalted as Lord of all. This common core of christian faith is expressed with differing emphases in different books. There is both unity and variety.

We are all inclined to have our favourite parts of the New Testament. Some of us are attracted to Paul, others to the gospels. Some, perhaps, are suspicious of 'complicated theology' and prefer the uncomplicated directness of the letter of James. And having chosen our favourites, we either interpret everything else in the light of them, or we simply keep everything else at the bottom of our reading lists. But taking the New Testament seriously means taking its variety seriously, listening to the different messages which come from different books.

Take James and Paul, for instance. It is well known that there is an apparent contradiction between Paul's stress on salvation or 'justification' through faith alone, and James' assertion that it is by his actions that a person is put right with God, and not by his faith alone (James 2.24). The temptation here is to say, 'Well, there isn't really a contradiction, because Paul is telling us that we cannot come to God except by faith, whilst James is saying that our faith has to result in action'. So the contradiction is resolved, our theological system remains intact, with its ends neatly tied.

The trouble with such a procedure is that it protects us from the *force* of what both James and Paul are saying. Do we sometimes wonder if God can accept us? Are we tempted to think that because of our tradition or our goodness we have some special claim on God? Then we need to hear undiluted Paul's declaration that by God's grace we can come to him, we must come to him with nothing but the open hand of faith. Do we sometimes imagine that we are secure in our orthodoxy, that God is pleased with us because we believe the right things? Then we need to feel the cold blast of James' attack on that 'faith without works' which is utterly dead.

Different New Testament books show us different facets of God's truth. If we ignore the richness of that variety, we do so to our own poverty.

Summary

This chapter has opened up two very different books.

From our study of Acts we saw the dangers of assuming that a biblical narrative always offers examples for the church to follow. We should model ourselves and our churches on what Luke describes only where he shows that it is his intention to provide a model. Hence it is important, as in the case of a gospel, to look for recurrent themes and particular emphases.

Revelation introduces us to churches under threat of persecution, and invites us to see the purpose of God being worked out even through the suffering of God's people. In a book such as this, it is more important to see the book as a whole, to sense the drama unfolding chapter by chapter, than to analyse every verse in detail.

The difference between these and other New Testament books is to be welcomed. Different books speak to different circumstances. But for each of us, a willingness to listen to the New Testament's different voices broadens our horizons and preserves our faith from self-indulgence.

Questions for discussion

1 In this chapter it was suggested that the main message of the Acts of the Apostles can be summarized under four headings (pages 73–75). What – if anything – might each of these themes imply for the mission of your church?

2 Study Acts 10.34–43, in which Luke summarizes the gospel preached by Peter to Cornelius. What do you think are the most important features of Peter's message? Should gospel-preaching today follow the same pattern?

3 Study Revelation 1.4–20. In what ways would the description of Christ in this passage help churches facing the prospect of persecution?

4 How can we best ensure that over a period of time we

listen to the variety of messages in different New Testament books? What should we do if different New Testament books appear to contradict each other?

6

How is the New Testament the word of God?

We come now to a group of questions which puzzle many people, and often lead to sharp disagreement. In what sense is the New Testament special? Why does the church regard these books as 'scripture', whilst ignoring other books written by early christians? What do we mean when we speak of the Bible's 'inspiration' and 'authority'?

Before exploring these issues, I can refrain no longer from emphasizing that the New Testament – the subject of this book – is only part of the christian Bible. In the end, of course, the New Testament can't be understood apart from the Old. It constantly quotes the Old Testament – over one thousand, six hundred times, someone has counted. The first christians saw the coming of Jesus, not as the replacement of jewish faith, but as the *fulfilment* of all that the jewish scriptures pointed to. Jesus saw himself and his mission in Old Testament terms – for example, as the suffering servant of God (Isaiah 53; Mark 10.45), and as the one endowed with the Holy Spirit to bring good news to the poor (Isaiah 61; Luke 4.18–21).

So if we are to understand Jesus, we find ourselves often driven back to the Old Testament. And when we stay with it for a while, we find all kinds of things there which are neither rejected nor repeated by the New Testament, but simply taken for granted. There is, for example, teaching about God, about ethical and social issues. There are expressions of worship (in the Psalms), reflections on everyday life (Proverbs) and on the mysteries of life (Job and Ecclesiastes). Since this book is about the New Testament, I shall say little more about the Old, though it will crop up occasionally in this chapter. But let it be underlined a thousand times, that our desire to understand the New Testament must, in due course, lead us to grapple with the Old.

Now let's return to our questions about the special character of the Bible. At first sight it seems odd to use words like 'inspired' to describe books produced by normal human processes. When introducing his gospel, Luke does not tell us that the Lord led him to write his book this way. He says he wrote it because it seemed a good idea, and he followed familiar painstaking methods of research. When Paul asks Timothy, 'Bring my coat that I left in Troas with Carpus' (2 Timothy 4.13), are we to call that inspired? Or consider 1 Corinthians 1.14–16, where Paul corrects himself as he goes along: 'I thank God that I did not baptize any of you except Crispus and Gaius . . . (Oh yes, I also baptized Stephanas and his family; but I can't remember whether I baptized anyone else).' If God were the real author of that, would he need to correct himself and confess his lack of memory?

And yet there *is* something special about the Bible. There is something about it which takes hold of people and leads them to the living God, as we saw at the beginning of chapter one. Like a supposedly extinct volcano, it has a way of unleashing its power even among those who have long thought it dead and ineffective. But most of us discover this 'specialness' of the Bible, not by listening to arguments about inspiration and authority, but through personal experience. We discover that through the Bible's message we encounter God. By it we are challenged, fed, encouraged. So it becomes, for us, the book we dare not do without when cast away on a desert island. How we think about the Bible, then, must take account of these two facts about it. It is clearly a human book, produced by human processes, reflecting human personalities. But it is also a book which has God behind it and leads us to him.

An inspired book

To say that the Bible is inspired does not mean simply that it is inspiring, like other great literature. If we say no more than that about it, we underplay God's involvement in its creation. And we are left without adequate explanation of why it has so consistently, in so many different cultures, had such a life-changing influence on people. On the other hand, inspiration cannot mean that God has 'dictated' the contents of the biblical books, reducing their authors to the level of mere typewriters, passive receivers and transmitters of words from on high. For we have already noticed the very human processes by which biblical books were produced. We have seen how Paul's letters reflect his human personality, just as the personality that we glimpse behind the pages of Jeremiah is different from the personality of Ezekiel. We cannot give up the conviction that biblical books are human books, any more than we can give up insisting that Jesus was human, a jew of a particular period, with a particular personality. So what do we mean by inspiration?

The term appears in 2 Timothy 3.16: 'All scripture is inspired by God . . .' The Greek word for 'inspired by God' was sometimes used to describe wisdom or dreams which were believed to come from God. 2 Timothy is therefore claiming that all scripture (meaning, of course, the Old Testament, since the New Testament did not yet exist) is of divine origin. But the passage does not tell us what the relation is between its divine origin and human authorship.

This basic statement is filled out by the claims which biblical authors sometimes make for themselves, and by the attitude to the Old Testament which we find in Jesus and the New Testament writers. Old Testament prophets were particularly conscious of receiving their messages from God. 'The Lord said to me . . .' (Jeremiah 1.4). 'The Sovereign Lord says . . .' (Jeremiah 1.20). Paul gives a judgement about marriage, and adds: 'That is my opinion, and I think that I too have God's Spirit' (1 Corinthians 7.40).

It is striking how frequently Jesus appeals to the Old Testament with a clear indication that he attributes divine origin and divine authority to the passage in question. After reminding some pharisees of a passage in Isaiah, he comments, 'You put aside God's command and obey the teachings of men' (Mark 7.6–8). When asked about divorce, he quotes Genesis 2.24 about man and woman becoming one, and introduces it with the formula, 'God said', even though in Genesis God is not represented as the actual speaker (Matthew 19.5). For Jesus, what scripture says, God says. The Old Testament shaped his understanding of God and his will, and of his own mission. Even when he spoke of particular texts as being in some sense superseded by his own coming, as in the contrasts of Matthew 5.21–48 ('You have heard that it was said . . . but now I tell you . . .'), he never suggested that those texts had not come from God. He showed *both* a respect for scripture's God-given authority, *and* a creative freedom in applying it to the new situation brought about through his ministry.

But how does this help us with the New Testament? Jesus may have spoken of the inspiration of the Old Testament, but he didn't set his seal of approval on the New Testament, unwritten as it was during his ministry. However, there are some indications as to why it shouldn't be regarded simply as a collection of human documents. First, it is natural that the God who provided the Old Testament would complement it with documents which bear witness to its fulfilment in Jesus. Secondly, New Testament documents themselves make claims which have to be taken seriously. As we have seen, the same letters of Paul, which contain routine information about travel and greetings from secretaries, also express a consciousness of divine direction in the guidance which the letters offer. Paul, like other New Testament letter writers, is conscious of his apostleship, his divine commission to build churches on the foundation which is Christ (1 Corinthians 3.10–11). The chief purpose of apostles was to bear witness to the facts, the meaning and the implications of Christ's work. The New Testament scriptures, which come from apostles and from people close to them, are special because these apostles were commissioned by Christ himself.

John's gospel includes the promise that the Holy Spirit would remind the disciples of all that Jesus had said (John 14.26). The author probably believed that this was precisely what was happening, as he expressed in his gospel the significance of Jesus' words and deeds.

None of this, however, tells us *how* the inspiration of biblical books took place. It may be helpful for us to think of the Bible rather as we think of Christ – as being both human and divine. We cannot say *how* these elements are combined, but we can affirm that both elements are there. Perhaps the creation of a gospel or one of Paul's letters is not so different in kind – though different in degree – from the production of a sermon. When a preacher prepares a sermon, there is the process of study and thought which is often complex and frustrating. But there are also the flashes of insight, the God-given message for this particular congregation, which can make the sermon a 'word from the Lord'. So when Luke writes a gospel there is the research, the sifting of evidence, the organizing of material. When Paul writes a letter, there is the application of hard thinking to particular issues. But in both cases there is the Holy Spirit working through the writing process so that the intended readers receive what *God* wants them to hear.

We can't prove that the Bible is inspired. We can argue that it is reasonable to expect that the kind of God who is revealed in Jesus wouldn't leave us floundering for the truth about him. We can show how seriously Jesus regarded the Old Testament, and what claims various biblical writers made for their writings. But we can't prove that those claims are true. In the end it's a matter of faith – our own faith, and the faith of the church down the ages. Recognizing that something is God's word is an act of spiritual discernment, of personal response.

Inspiration and interpretation

If I recognize the New Testament as inspired by God, that doesn't solve all my problems about scripture. For example, I cannot say, 'Because the Bible is inspired, therefore it is factually accurate in every respect'. It would certainly seem inconceivable that, if God inspired biblical writers, he would deliberately mislead them and us. But complete factual or historical accuracy doesn't necessarily follow from inspiration. It's all a question of what *kind* of accuracy, what *kind* of information, God intended to give us through the biblical writers. So we have to study the documents themselves to try to establish what the authors intended. Now, we have already seen, when we looked at the gospels, how the authors adapted their material, told it from different points of view, even altered minor points of detail. So our understanding of inspiration must take account of the fact that biblical writers were apparently not concerned about minute historical accuracy. Failure to grasp this point has even led one writer to suggest that Peter must have denied Jesus six times if all the gospel accounts, with their slight variations, are to be fitted together.

Another example of the kind of difficulty which has to be taken on board *with* our understanding of inspiration is the sometimes peculiar ways in which New Testament writers quote the Old Testament. I remember one bible study group meeting when a young man's trust in the Bible was severely shaken by his study of Ephesians 4.8. The discussion here of spiritual gifts quotes Psalm 68.18:

> When he went up to the very heights,
> he took many captives with him;
> he gave gifts to mankind.

But when he looked up the Psalm in the Old Testament, this man noticed that it says not 'he gave gifts' but 'he received gifts from rebellious men'. It looks as though Paul has turned the meaning upside-down to suit his own purposes.

Before accusing Paul of being arbitrary in his treatment of the Old Testament, we must recall that New Testament writers normally quoted from memory. They didn't own a copy of the scriptures which they could look up whenever necessary. And there was already a paraphrase of the Psalms in Aramaic (the everyday language of Palestine) which also said 'gave' rather than 'received'. Paul appears to be calling this paraphrase to mind – rather like a modern preacher citing a particular translation of the Bible which brings out a point he wishes to make. This may not seem to us the most careful and proper way to handle an Old Testament text. But it is the way New Testament writers do sometimes use the Old Testament, and our doctrine of inspiration has to be flexible enought to cope with it.

And belief in inspiration doesn't solve problems of interpretation. My belief that the Letter to the Hebrews is inspired by God doesn't automatically make it any easier to understand. I still have to work at it in the way we thought about in chapter four. Some things in it may remain unclear, some may be open to dispute. But my belief in its inspiration will commit me to grappling with awkward questions and difficult passages. For if it is God's word I can hardly treat it with anything less than a real seriousness. Belief in inspiration certainly does not justify me in looking for short-cuts to the meaning of a passage, or indulging in 'blessed thoughts' which bear little relation to the author's intention and his readers' situation.

Why these particular books?

Why do we attribute divine inspiration to the twenty-seven books of the New Testament, and not to more, or less? This is the question of the New Testament canon. Pressure for the early church to establish a canon – a collection of recognized writings whose authority was recognized – came from two main sources. *Within* the church, missionary expansion highlighted the need for authoritative accounts of Jesus' ministry and apostolic guidance for young churches. The death of apostles by the end of the first century increased the sense that apostolic teaching should be preserved for the benefit of later generations. *Outside* the church, heretics in the second century began to use – and misuse – christian literature. Around AD 150 one heretic called Marcion drew up a list of books, including Luke's gospel and Paul's letters, of which he approved – though he cut out from them allusions to the Old Testament of which he thoroughly disapproved. Provoked in this way, more orthodox christians could hardly fail to feel the need of their own 'official' list of writings.

The development of the canon proceeded in an apparently haphazard manner. The four gospels and the letters of Paul were generally accepted as authoritative by the second half of the second century, and the letters of Peter, James and John were soon widely used. But christians in different areas had their own favourites among these and other books bearing titles such as the Shepherd of Hermas, the Gospel of Peter, and the Epistle of Barnabas. We are not to imagine a conference of bishops or bible scholars, solemnly sitting round a table and voting which books should be in the New Testament and which not. There never was such a conference. The process of selection grew out of the church's life. It was the 'grass roots' who formed the canon as they used the books and found some to be more valuable than others. Eventually the twenty-seven books of our New Testament emerged as those which had stood the test of time and experience. From the fourth century onwards, the contents of the canon were universally acknowledged.

On what grounds were these books accepted, and others rejected? In sifting the documents, the christians of the second and third centuries seem to have had three 'tests' in mind. First, they asked of a document, Is it apostolic? Does it come from an apostle, or from someone close to an apostle? The letters of Paul and Peter passed this test, as did the gospels of Matthew and John, which were believed to be written by apostles. Mark's gospel was accepted because it was believed to express the preaching of Peter, and Luke's gospel and Acts because of Luke's close association with Paul. On the other hand, there were people who rejected the Revelation of John because its author could hardly be the same person who wrote the gospel of John, which breathes a very different air.

This test of apostolic origin is something of an embarrassment in modern times, because many scholars have seen reason to question whether apostles actually wrote some of the books attributed to them. Few think Matthew wrote the gospel which bears his name. For why should an eyewitness of Jesus' ministry use Mark, who was not an eyewitness, as his source? Yet some of the material in Matthew which does not come from Mark *may* derive from the apostle. Few people believe that Paul wrote Hebrews – and his name doesn't appear in the text of the letter – yet Hebrews came to be accepted in the canon largely because it was thought to be by Paul. A greater problem is presented to us by the claim of some scholars that letters such as Ephesians, 1 and 2 Timothy and Titus, are not by Paul; and 2 Peter is not by Peter.

To this we might respond that even if not by the apostles themselves, these letters come from people close to the apostles who understood the apostles' minds and so meet the test of apostolic origin as readily as do Mark and Luke. But, more importantly, apostolic authorship was never the only, or even the major, factor in determining whether a book was canonical. Serapion, bishop of Antioch in the late second-century, was asked if the Gospel of Peter could be treated as authoritative in his church. He said yes, on the grounds of apostolic authorship. But later, when he had read it, he withdrew his approval because the *content* showed that apostolic authorship was a fake.

The second test, then, was about content. Does the book conform to the truth of Christ as we have been taught it? Through argument with heretics like Marcion, Christian leaders developed a good nose for distinguishing between heresy and the essential truths of the gospel. They rejected books which denied that Christ was truly God and truly man. So, despite the variety of emphasis among books that are in the New Testament, there were clearly limits to what was acceptable.

The third question, and the most decisive in the long run, was, Is the book useful for the Church's life? Maybe

Paul wrote a letter to Luke asking him to buy some olives and book a passage on a ship. That would be apostolic and perfectly orthodox. But it would hardly be useful to the church, so it is not preserved and not in the canon! The books that are there are those which, over several generations, proved their usefulness for teaching and renewing the church's life. The gospels reveal Jesus of Nazareth, the focus of christian faith. The letters interpret his significance in the light of the resurrection, and hammer out guidelines for christian living. Acts portrays the church as God's agent in proclaiming Christ. Revelation assures the church of the ultimate triumph of God's purpose in Christ.

We need to remind ourselves that the New Testament has proved itself in the *church's* experience, whenever we are tempted to think about it in too individualistic a way. Suppose someone says, 'But this part of the Bible leaves me cold', or 'I can't see why that book is in the Bible'. Part of the answer is that we belong to a church which has valued these books, and our own spiritual life and insight is the poorer if we don't try to understand *why* it has been valued. If the letter of Jude means little to many christians today, is that because we are too soft on false teaching in the church? If Revelation makes us impatient, we can remind ourselves that this book has often been vitally important to christians facing persecution. That may not automatically bring Revelation to life for us, but reading it will make us sensitive to the suffering church which draws great strength from it.

The authority of the New Testament

Because the New Testament is inspired by God, because it has proved its worth as the book which brings people into touch with God and holds them there, we speak of its *authority*. This authority is not a weapon with which to beat people over the head, like the authority of a dictator. It is more like the authority of a wise counsellor whose advice we have learnt to trust through experience – so that, even when he says things which puzzle us or make us uncomfortable, we are inclined to trust his judgement.

The New Testament's authority is derived from the authority of Christ. Because we submit to Jesus as Lord and recognize his authority over us, we want to take seriously all that he says to us. And we find this not only in the gospels but in the other New Testament books which embody the teaching of people commissioned by him to explain and interpret him. For them there is simply no substitute. We don't deny the importance of the church's tradition down the centuries. We don't reject the insights which come from our God-given reason, from the discoveries of science and from secular thought. We don't deny that God sometimes speaks directly to people's minds today. But as an authoritative witness to Christ and his will, the New Testament is the best we have. We can't get closer to the Christ who lived and died and lives again that we get through those pages. That is why we call the New Testament our supreme authority. However, if we take biblical authority seriously, there is a question we cannot duck.

Does it all have authority for us today?

A tricky question posed for us, particularly by the New Testament letters, is the problem of cultural relativity. That is, how do we know what parts of their message have *permanent* relevance, and what parts applied only in their first-century culture? For cultures and customs vary from one society to another, from one period to another. And it is not automatically appropriate to transfer to our culture teaching which was originally addressed to another culture. Even christians who are inclined to take every command of scripture with literal seriousness don't normally take slavery for granted. Nor do most of them heed Paul's instruction, 'Are you unmarried? Then don't look for a wife' (1 Corinthians 7.27).

Because the letters were written to specific situations and were not dropped from heaven in a timeless package, it is right to see some elements in them as intended only for those who first received them. Nobody doubts that this is the case with 1 Corinthians 16.10: 'If Timothy comes your way, be sure to make him feel welcome among you.' Equally, everyone agrees that Paul's passage about love in 1 Corinthians 13 has significance for us and for all time.

But what about all the passages which fall somewhere between these clear-cut examples? Why do some Christians insist that women should cover their heads during worship, as 1 Corinthians 11 says, whilst others regard that passage as applying only to the first-century? Should wives submit to their husbands (Ephesians 5.22–24)? Should christians always 'greet one another with a brotherly kiss' (1 Corinthians 16.20)? It is very tempting to pick from the New Testament those teachings which are congenial to us, and to dismiss uncomfortable passages as relevant only to the first century. We need guidelines which will enable us to be *consistent* in our handling of the question of cultural relativity. I do not imagine that the following guidelines will settle all debates, but I think they can help us towards a more consistent and responsible treatment of awkward passages.

1 Try to distinguish between what the New Testament writers themselves regard as central, and what they regard as less important or more variable. In the area of doctrine, for example, themes such as people's need of

God's forgiveness, the grace of God for salvation through the death and resurrection of Jesus, the unique status of Jesus as God's way of bringing people to himself – these are consistently emphasized through the New Testament. On the other hand, there seems to have been considerable variety over how the church and its ministry were structured in different New Testament churches. And this suggests that no one pattern is the true God-given pattern to the exclusion of all others.

In a similar way, New Testament teaching about behaviour consistently emphasizes that love for all people is the christian's essential calling, and urges christians not to retaliate against personal attacks. It argues that sins such as idolatry, foul language, adultery, homosexual activity, greed are always wrong. Lists of sins (such as those in 1 Corinthians 6.9–10; Galatians 5.19–21; Ephesians 5.3–5) frequently include such items. But matters which might be relative to one culture or another – whether to drink alcohol, for example, or whether women should cover their heads at worship – are never mentioned in such lists, and seem to be less important.

As we saw in the last chapter, there are several issues on which the New Testament does not speak with a single voice. Apart from the various approaches to the Church's ministry, there are different views about such matters as whether the Roman state is an agent of God or of Satan (Romans 13.1–7; 1 Peter 2.13–14; Revelation 13), or whether christians should give away their money and possessions (Luke 12.33; 18.22; 1 Timothy 6.17–19). The problem about meat sacrificed to idols, which we studied in chapter four, gets a different answer in Acts 15.29 and Revelation 2.14, 20. These differences might be accounted for by differing insights of different authors. Or they might be responses to the particular circumstances of different individuals. This certainly seems the most likely reason for Jesus' radical command to the rich man in Luke 18.22. Or the different emphases may reflect the differing circumstances addressed by the various writers. Revelation 13 takes a more negative view of the state than Romans 13, because it is written amidst the threat of widespread persecution. Acts 15 and Revelation 2 are less flexible, more negative about the possibility of eating meat offered to idols, because their context requires them to give more weight to jewish scruples.

By being alert to such questions about what the New Testament itself treats as central, and what it regards as secondary or variable, we can begin to discern which parts were meant only for particular first-century contexts and which parts have authority for us.

2 Recognize the distinction within the New Testament between a general principle and a specific application. Sometimes a writer can use a general principle – which is not relative to a particular culture – to support a specific application to one particular culture or situation. For instance, in that notoriously difficult passage about covering the head in worship, Paul appeals to the divine order of creation in support of his argument (1 Corinthians 11.3). But that appeal to a general principle doesn't necessarily make the specific teaching about covering the head applicable to all circumstances and all cultures. Equally, I might support the view that it's OK to drink wine by appealing to the general principle, 'The earth and everything in it belong to the Lord' (Psalm 24.1 – which Paul appeals to in 1 Corinthians 10.26). But that would not justify me in asserting that to drink wine is right for all people in all circumstances.

In 1 Corinthians 11, Paul in fact gives signs that his instruction *is* relative to that situation, since he appeals to 'custom' or 'nature' (verses 13–16). In Paul's experience of what was normal, it was fair enough to say that 'nature itself teaches you that long hair on a man is a disgrace, but on a woman it is a thing of of beauty' (verses 14–15). But experience in different parts of the world shows that such distinctions in length of hair have more to do with cultural convention than with how human beings are made.

3 When faced with a passage which seems to be at odds with what you find elsewhere in the New Testament, take special care to study its background to see if there is some clear *reason* for what it says. This will involve use of commentaries. As a result, you may discover that the passage takes an unusual line on a topic because of the special circumstances it addresses. This method may *sound* like looking for a route to escape from the 'obvious' meaning of an uncongenial passage. But, in fact, it's a necessary part of taking seriously the fact that letters were addressed to specific situations.

1 Corinthians 11 is again our example here. There is some evidence from ancient Greek literature that men who wore long hair and women who wore short hair were thereby indicating that they were practising homosexuals. In that case, Paul is not laying down rules about haircuts and headcoverings for christians of all time. He is urging Corinthian christians, against that particular moral background, not to flaunt their new-found christian freedom in such a way as to cause misunderstanding and bring the gospel into disrepute. (For details, see J. Murphy-O'Connor, 'Sex and Logic in 1 Corinthians 11: 2–16', *Catholic Biblical Quarterly* 42 (1980), pp. 482–500).

4 Ask whether different cultural options were available to New Testament writers. If within their experience only one approach to a particular issue was available, then we are very likely dealing with something which is

relative to their culture rather than a ruling given for all time. For example, slavery was accepted as a normal part of society both among jews and in the Greek and Roman world. So it is not very surprising that New Testament writers don't advocate the abolition of slavery. Their failure to do so should not be taken to show that God intends slavery to exist until the end of time. The general thrust of biblical teaching, that every human being is of enormous value to God, and that 'you are all one in union with Christ Jesus' (Galatians 3.28), gradually led christians to see that slavery is incompatible with their faith.

Similarly, first-century women normally had no education and were generally regarded as inferior to men. They were simply useful for bearing children, running a home, and for sexual pleasure. Against this background, we should not be surprised at Paul's instruction to wives to submit to their husbands (Ephesians 5.22). Instead, we should notice with amazement that Paul places this in the context of everyone submitting to each other out of reverence for Christ (verse 21). And we should observe that Jesus and Paul both speak of the equality and mutual responsibility of man and woman – both in marriage and in the church (Mark 10.11–12; 1 Corinthians 7.3–4; 11.11–12; Galatians 3.28). Such ideas were virtually unheard of, and they show the direction in which the logic of christian insight was pointing.

Homosexuality, however, was a different matter. Missionaries such as Paul and the gentile churches which they founded, lived in a society where homosexual relationships were common and were approved by some eminent philosophers and opinion-formers. So, to approve of homosexual practice was an available option for New Testament writers. The fact that we only find strong disapproval of it (Romans 1.24–28; 1 Corinthians 6.9) – alongside strong affirmation of the God-given interdependence of men and women – pushes us to the conclusion that New Testament teaching on this matter is permanently valid.

5 Keep talking to those from whom you differ! With love and respect, try to establish *why* you differ. This may enable you to refine the principles suggested here, so that you can get into the issues more deeply and come closer to agreement. Though I disagree profoundly with some of my friends on matters of both belief and behaviour, I am bound by Paul's instruction: 'Accept one another, then, for the glory of God, as Christ has accepted you' (Romans 15.7). And *that* instruction is permanently valid, because it was given in a situation where people were disagreeing with each other (and so is comparable to the situation I am envisaging now); because it bases christians' acceptance of each other on Christ's acceptance of us; and because it is a specific instance of the universally applicable command to love.

Inspiration, authority and us

It is easy to get confused over the kind of issues we have discussed in this chapter. It is easy to get hot under the collar when other people's views differ from our own. It's then that we need the reminder that the point of our study is not simply to get our doctrine of scripture right, but to give scripture its right place in shaping our lives. In the passage we mentioned earlier, Paul's message to Timothy is, 'All Scripture is inspired by God and is useful for teaching the truth, rebuking error, correcting faults, and giving instruction for right living, so that the person who serves God may be fully qualified and equipped to do every kind of good deed' (2 Timothy 3.16–17). Understanding is important, but it must lead to a deepening relationship with Christ and a more Christ-like quality of life. And the Holy Spirit who inspired the writing of the scriptures brings light to our reading of them and power to live in obedience to them.

Summary

We began this chapter by observing that most christians discover the special nature of the New Testament through their experience of its impact on their lives. It was then suggested that its special nature is due to its being inspired by the Holy Spirit – though we cannot say exactly *how* this took place. We saw how the twenty-seven books of the New Testament came to be recognized as having special authority – mainly because of their consistent usefulness for the life of the church. Discussion of the New Testament's authority led to discussion of the problem of cultural relativity, and five guidelines were suggested for distinguishing teaching which was specifically for New Testament times, from that which has permanent validity.

Questions for discussion

1 'Because we submit to Jesus as Lord and recognize his authority over us, we want to take seriously all that he says to us' (page 97). Do you agree that submission to Jesus as Lord commits us to accepting the authority of the New Testament over our lives?

2 How would you respond to the person who says, 'Because the Bible is the word of God it must be literally true'?

3 Study Colossians 3.18 to 4.1. Using the five guidelines explained in the last part of this chapter, can you suggest which of these instructions have authority for us, and which may be no longer valid?

7

The New Testament and christian belief

So far in this book we've started from the New Testament itself and asked questions about how to understand it. In this and the next two chapters we shall sometimes start from *our* end, our questions. For example, we may want to ask, What am I to believe about Jesus Christ? How can the New Testament help me when I find prayer difficult? Does the New Testament give any guidance about test-tube babies or the rights and wrongs of industrial strikes? In such cases we begin not with a book or passage of the Bible but with an issue, and we ask what parts of scripture might direct our thinking about it.

In this chapter we ask questions about what christians believe. How is christian doctrine built on the New Testament? How do we ensure that the content of our faith is genuinely faithful to the New Testament? Now there are people who question the very idea that 'christian doctrine' can be constructed by drawing together teachings from the various New Testament writers. They point to the very different emphases to be found in various New Testament books, and the fact that even a single writer, such as Paul, can say very different things in different places. And they say that any attempt to mix these elements together to make 'the New Testament doctrine of salvation', or of anything else, is misguided. It is an attempt to create a doctrinal system out of varied material which cannot be reduced to a system. It is like trying to fit together pieces from several small jigsaws into one large and coherent picture.

Now I have, myself, stressed the different emphases of different books, and have shown how different situations call forth different responses from Paul. But I don't think this makes it wrong or impossible to talk about 'New Testament theology' or 'christian doctrine'. For although Paul says different things in different letters – he doesn't write 'systemic theology' – there is a *coherence* about his thought. He doesn't just throw up ideas as they occur to him and then drop them in favour of something else. There are common threads running through his letters, for example about the person of Christ, the christian hope, the Holy Spirit and the nature of salvation.

Paul mentions to the church in Rome (where he himself has not yet been) 'the truths found in the teaching you received' (Romans 6.17). This suggests that there was a core of basic teaching shared by different teachers (including Paul) in different christian churches. This is supported by the fact that New Testament letters several times quote creeds or hymns which expressed the heart of the faith of the churches which used them. Paul is quoting from such a creed in Romans 1.3–4, about Jesus' humanity and his status as Son of God. Longer examples of creeds or hymns – it is not always easy to tell the difference – are 1 Corinthians 15.3–5; Philippians 2.6–11, 1 Timothy 3.16. So despite the varieties of New Testament faith, which we must not lose sight of, there is a shared faith focused on Jesus Christ, risen from the dead, the unique Saviour.

Right and wrong approaches

There are a number of dangers to avoid, and guidelines to follow, in building doctrines on the New Testament. The basic guideline is to hold on to the lessons we have learnt in earlier chapters. We shall not have good doctrine if we do not have careful interpretation of what the New Testament says, taking account of its context and content. We must keep listening to what a New Testament writer wants to say and why he wants to say it. We must not assume that we can jump straight from what a text says to what it means for us, without giving thought to the differences between the New Testament world and our world. We must ask how our understanding of the inspiration and authority of scripture affects our attitude to doctrines expressed in scripture. If we take notice of such guidelines we shall avoid certain dangers.

One danger is an over-eagerness to divide biblical teaching up into neat compartments which suit *our* doctrinal systems but dismember a biblical writer's argument in the process. It is tempting to us, for example, to put Romans 12.1–2 into a compartment labelled 'spirituality', verses 3–8 into one marked 'church and ministry', and verses 9–21 into the compartment of 'christian behaviour'. The fact is that for Paul they form a developing argument on themes which he sees as being in very close relation. Similarly Colossians 3.12–17 mixes together what we would be inclined to divide into doctrine, ethics, spirituality and worship. We distort biblical doctrine if we use a doctrinal text without respect for its context in the biblical author's argument.

At its worst, of course, such use of texts without respect for the context is the approach known as 'appealing to proof-texts'. A biblical text is used as a peg on which to hang a doctrine which may well have been arrived at for various questionable reasons. For example, some strands of charismatic Christianity emphasize 'baptism in the Spirit' as an experience which God offers to christians at some later stage than the beginning of their christian life. But if the six passages which refer to 'baptism in the Spirit' (Matthews 3.11; Mark 1.8; Luke 3.16; Acts 1.5; 11.16; 1 Corinthians 12.13) are read in context, they can hardly refer to an experience later than conversion. Acts 11.16, for example, refers to Cornelius' experience of the Holy

Spirit at his *first* encounter with the christian gospel. And Paul in 1 Corinthians 12.13 says that *all* christians 'have been baptized into the one body by the same Spirit'. Incidentally, I am not denying that the experiences labelled 'baptism in the Spirit' are genuine experiences from God. I am simply urging that 'baptism in the Spirit' is an unbiblical label to put on them.

But while we must allow New Testament writers to express christian faith in their own terms and we must study what they say in context, christian doctrine for us cannot be simply a repetition of New Testament words. Within the New Testament itself there is development of doctrine. Paul, for example, developed his understanding of the person of Christ as new questions were raised which had to be thought through. Paul and John particularly adapted their ways of expressing the faith as the Church moved from a jewish world into a predominantly Greek world. Rather than use Jesus' own peculiarly jewish term for himself, 'Son of man', they favoured titles like 'Son of God' and 'Lord'.

This kind of development had to go on, as christians thought about their faith in the light of new questions and new situations. Most obviously, perhaps, the doctrine of the Trinity is not clearly stated in the New Testament. But the raw materials are there in the way that the approach of God to man is constantly spoken of in a three-fold form. For example, Paul speaks in 2 Corinthians 13.13 of 'the grace of the Lord Jesus Christ, the love of God, and the fellowship of the Holy Spirit'. And Ephesians 1.3–14 weaves together references to the work of Father, Son and Spirit in our salvation. The first christians' experience of God led them to speak of Father, Son and Spirit in divine terms, and the implications of this led inevitably to the doctrine of the Trinity. Ernest Rutherford split the atom in a Cambridge laboratory in 1918, but the implications of that discovery continued to be worked out in later years. So it is with the christian faith. The essential revelation is there in the New Testament, but the implications go on being worked out and expressed afresh.

But of course when we talk about doctrine developing we do not mean that there are no controls on how the development occurs. We have to ask whether any particular 'development' is *consistent* with the biblical witness. I know one theologian, for instance, who claims that there is no place in modern christianity for belief in life after death. But this assertion surely stands in such sharp opposition to a fundamental conviction, based on the resurrection of Jesus, of all New Testament writers, that it can hardly be entertained as a legitimately christian view.

Another danger in the development of doctrine is that a piece of biblical teaching comes to be interpreted in terms of the interpreter's theological tradition or denominational viewpoint. Ask a baptist, a roman catholic and a Greek orthodox christian how they understand the significance of Jesus' words, 'This is my body' (Mark 14.22), and you will appreciate how our understanding of the New Testament can be coloured by the traditions within which we are nurtured. This is why it is so important to recognize the *distance* between us and the New Testament world of which we spoke in chapter one. Sometimes we have to strip away the assumptions built into our various traditions if we are to respond to what the text really means instead of what we have always assumed it meant.

Being sensitive to the distance between us and the New Testament world also means that we can't always take its doctrinal content at face value. In periods when the idea of a three-decker universe was generally accepted, christians were inclined to take literally the story of Jesus' ascension. He went upwards to heaven because God is up there. Now that our view of the universe, and of God's relationship to it, is less simple than that, we have to understand the story more symbolically. In telling the story (Acts 1.6–11) Luke is affirming that the resurrection appearances of Christ had now come to an end, and that he now shared in God's rule over the world. The cloud (verse 9) is of course regularly a symbol in the Bible of God's presence.

More difficult is the question of how we handle the stories in the gospels about Jesus' exorcisms. Does our 'modern world view' rule out the possibility that Jesus was really casting out real demons, and that christians may, on occasion, be called to do the same thing today? Some people point to the similarities between the description of the 'boy with an evil spirit', in Mark 9.14–29, and the characteristics of an epileptic fit. And they say that to attribute the symptoms to an evil spirit is a primitive way of explaining what we now understand in terms of medical science. And yet those christians today who are involved in exorcism and in ministry to people who have been involved with the occult often testify to a sense of the power of evil which confronts them in their work. I do not think this sense of evil can be so easily dismissed in the name of modern medical science. We may be hesitant about much traditional and popular language about the devil. And we should certainly reject – as the New Testament itself does – the idea that every illness or misfortune is a manifestation of demonic influence. But the biblical insistence that there is a power of evil in the world which is more than the total of evil in human individuals, demands to be taken seriously. It can't simply be side-stepped on grounds of 'cultural relativity'.

Taking scripture as God's word

If we believe in the inspiration and authority of the New

Testament in the way described in chapter six, three implications follow. In the first place, because the same God is behind it all, we expect to find a basic unity in what it teaches. Despite all I have said about the variety of scripture, the unity is remarkable. Christian doctrine involves drawing together the witness of different parts of the New Testament on a particular theme, so as to build a balanced and comprehensive understanding of that theme. If I wish to develop a christian understanding of healing, I can't do it by turning only to stories of Jesus' healings and exorcisms in the New Testament. I must also enquire about the biblical doctrine of creation, for this is the proper basis for affirming the value of medicine: medical healing and 'divine healing' in response to prayer are activities of the one creating and saving God. And I must see if the New Testament offers examples of people who are *not* healed, despite being prayed for (answer: yes, probably – Paul in 2 Corinthians 12.7–10; Trophimus in 2 Timothy 4.20). The reason for this lack of immediate healing is not to be sought in slogans like, 'You didn't pray hard enough' or 'There must be unconfessed sin in your life'. It lies rather in the New Testament's perspective on the kingdom of God: God's perfect kingdom where evil and suffering are abolished has been introduced *in part* by the coming of Jesus, but will not *fully* come until the final 'day of the Lord', which remains in the future. Meanwhile, the *presence* of God's kingdom means that healing is a real possibility, but the fact that its presence is as yet *incomplete* means that healing is not guaranteed. Such an understanding of healing from a christian perspective (*very* briefly summarized here) cannot be got from isolated proof-texts but only from reflection on the picture which is built up from different strands of New Testament teaching.

A second implication of our understanding of the nature of scripture, is that we take seriously teaching which we find hard to accept. Even when – or especially when – we find a doctrine uncomfortable, we bow to it because it is God's word to us and not just a human opinion. Biblical teaching about God's judgement is an example of this. None of us *likes* the doctrine. Probably all of us would prefer it not to be there. Yet there it is – and more frequent on Jesus' lips than in most of the rest of the New Testament. It is so closely bound up with Jesus' understanding of God that we cannot detach it without distorting what is central to his message.

Now, when I say of a doctrine, 'We bow to it because it is God's word to us', I am not abandoning my argument in chapter six about 'cultural relativity'. As I argued then, some things taught in the New Testament were taught for specific first century situations and don't apply to our situation. But the doctrine of judgement does not pass the tests suggested there for deciding that a message applies only to the first century situation. In particular, it is taught in such a wide variety of New Testament books and contexts that it is clearly part of the bedrock of New Testament faith. And it is not the case that no alternative view of human destiny was available to the biblical writers: a variety of ideas was discussed both in the jewish world and in the Greek world. But Jesus and the earliest christians affirmed consistently that God holds human beings accountable for their lives, and will one day underline the choices we have made, whether to live in God's way and seek his presence, or to resist him and flee from him. We may still have questions about an uncomfortable doctrine such as this, but if we try to submit to it and grapple with it, we may begin to understand why it is there. For instance, the teaching that God holds us all to account, safeguards the truth that God treats all our actions as significant and respects the choices which we make. If there were no judgement, then ultimately none of our actions would be significant. Our importance as responsible human beings would be vastly reduced.

Thirdly, our respect for scripture means that we keep listening for what scripture treats as important. So often *our* interests, *our* concerns, distort our approach to the New Testament. We read Paul's letter to the Romans mostly as an explanation of individual salvation, because that is what interests us. But the burning issue for Paul at the heart of Romans (chapter 9–11) is the problem of the jews' rejection of Jesus, and God's ultimate purpose for jews and gentiles. And this concern is there in the announcement that the gospel is for jews and gentiles alike (1.16), and in the insistence that 'there is no difference' in God's treatment of jew and gentile (3.22; 10.12). Our tendency to treat Romans 9–11 as a rather complicated digression is to miss at least half the point of the letter. This is not to dismiss our concerns and questions as unimportant. But if our reading of the Bible is always dominated by our concerns, we risk only finding in it the things we want to find, and our vision of God and his purposes will remain small.

Three examples

Let us now look briefly at three issues in doctrine which, I believe, must be handled in different ways in order to do justice to our guidelines for interpreting the New Testament. The first issue is one on which there is a clear and substantial unity among the New Testament writers: the nature of Jesus' resurrection. Now it is sometimes argued that, whilst all the New Testament writers affirm the resurrection, their belief about it takes many different forms. For instance, although the gospel writers tell stories which report that, on the Sunday after his crucifixion, Jesus' tomb was found empty, Paul makes no mention of the empty tomb. For him – and therefore, it is implied, for us – the empty tomb is irrelevant. What mattered was the conviction of Jesus' 'livingness', made real by his resurrection appearances. We can believe in the resurrection of Jesus without necessarily believing that his physical body was raised from the tomb.

Now I would argue that such an account of the matter fails to do justice to the unity of the New Testament witness to Jesus' resurrection. To argue that belief in the empty tomb is optional because only the gospels refer to it, implies a take-it-or-leave-it attitude to the witness of the gospels. And it involves questionable assumptions about what the rest of the New Testament writers believed. Of course, I am not suggesting that resurrection is simply the restoring of a dead man to physical life, like the raising of Lazarus in John 11. Nor am I saying that the empty tomb proves that Jesus rose from the dead. Undoubtedly, it was the appearances of the risen Lord which convinced his disciples that he was victorious over death. As the gospels themselves show, the empty tomb on its own was simply a puzzle, open to various explanations (Matthew 28.11–15; Luke 24.1–12; John 20.1–15). But the empty tomb is important because it is the visible demonstration that God really raised Jesus from death, and that the resurrection appearances were no mere hallucinations or subjective experiences in the minds of the disciples. It was not the disciples' experiences which produced faith in the resurrection: it was the resurrection of Jesus which produced the experiences and created faith.

Whilst it is true that Paul does not mention the empty tomb, he does *imply* that the tomb was empty. In 1 Corinthians 15 he summarizes his gospel message, 'that Christ died . . . , that he was buried and that he was raised to life . . .' (verses 3–4). There would be no point mentioning the burial unless it was meant to imply that between the burial and the appearances on the third day, something happened to the buried body. In fact, for a first-century jew, the term 'resurrection' couldn't fail to involve the idea of the body itself being raised to life. It meant much more than the persistence of a person's influence or the immortality of his soul. And when the apostles began proclaiming the resurrection seven weeks after Jesus' death, and within a few hundred yards of his tomb, opponents would inevitably have produced evidence that his body remained in it – if there was any such evidence.

So it is part of the central New Testament faith in the risen Christ that Jesus' tomb was empty on the third day, and that his resurrection involved the raising and transformation of his body. His resurrection was not a series of events experienced by his disciples, but an act of God, something which happened to Jesus and was then revealed to his disciples. In their different ways, the New Testament writers affirm this central truth.

Having recognized the centrality of this resurrection for christian faith, we may give due weight to the variety with which New Testament writers work out its implications for us. Luke, for example, in his story of the Emmaus road, presents the risen Christ as one who walks with us along the way and meets us in the Lord's Supper (Luke 24.13–35). John, Paul and Peter proclaim that his triumph over death ensures triumph over death for his followers (John 11.25–26; 1 Corinthians 15.20–22; 1 Peter 1.3–4). Paul also explains how God's power, which raised Jesus from death, is also the power which enables us to live a new, Christ-like life (Romans 6.1–11). And the author of Revelation declares that Christ, 'the first to be raised from death', is also 'the ruler of the kings of the world' (Revelation 1.5). These are different messages to meet different needs, different situations. But all of these are based on the central affirmation that 'on the third day he rose again from the dead'.

Patterns of church life

The nature and centrality of Christ's resurrection, then, is an issue on which the New Testament writers show a remarkable degree of unity. And our commitment to the New Testament's authority requires us to show the same unity. In contrast, New Testament teaching about the church and its ministry shows remarkable variety, and our commitment to scripture requires us to take that variety seriously. Perhaps nothing has hampered the ecumenical movement more than the insistence that, if progress is to be made, all churches must accept the three-fold order of bishops, priests and deacons. This pattern, though found in the second-century, is dubiously based in the New Testament. It has become institutionalized and fossilized. Insistence on it displays insensitivity to the rich variety of God's gifts of ministry to the church.

I am not suggesting that the church can ignore its past and begin again. I am suggesting that if we listened to the New Testament a little more than to church tradition, we might find God speaking to us a message of liberation. New Testament churches had various patterns of ministry, partly influenced by their social environment. The earliest church in Jerusalem was led by a group of apostles, who adapted their pattern of leadership as need arose – for example, by appointing the seven helpers to look after the needs of the Greek-speaking widows (Acts 6.1–7). According to Acts 14.23, Paul and Barnabas revisited each church founded on the first missionary journey, and appointed elders. They were following the familiar pattern of the synagogue, each of which had a 'board of elders'. In Corinth it was quite different. The church here was alive with charismatic gifts such as those listed in 1 Corinthians 12.4–11, 28–30. There is no hint that the Corinthian church had a fixed group of leaders. The picture is of a dynamic – and sometimes chaotic – community with all members playing their part in ministry to each other. The church to which the three letters of John are addressed was different again. No appointed leaders are mentioned, but charismatic gifts are not prominent either. It looks more like a house fellowship in which christians, dependent on Christ, teach each other and care for each other.

The differences between these churches arose partly from theological emphasis, and partly from their social context. But churches with different patterns of ministry did not dismiss each other as 'not proper churches' in the way that modern denominations often do. Nor did a church following one pattern set up a 'rival show' in a town alongside a church which had a different pattern. They accepted each other as sister churches and fellow-christians. Doctrine based on the New Testament will find ways of rejoicing in these varieties rather than bludgeoning churches into uniformity.

Another way in which our understanding of the church may be impoverished, is in the pictures by which we think of the church. For very many christians today, the main picture of the church is 'the body of Christ', which is found in Paul (1 Corinthians 12; Romans 12; Ephesians 4). The picture has become prominent as christians have learnt afresh that each of us has something vital to contribute to the church's life, and we are interdependent on each other, not dependent on one gifted leader.

However, we are in danger of forgetting that the New Testament has a whole host of pictures of the church; one scholar has counted ninety-six of them! This is important because our pictures of the church tend to determine how we view the church's task, and our own involvement in it. Any one picture taken on its own is illuminating and yet limited. That is why we need to be exposed to the full range of pictures available in the New Testament.

Thus the picture of the body of Christ sheds light in the way described above, and has led the way to spiritual renewal in many churches. Yet, on its own it risks emphasizing the internal relationships of members of the church at the expense of their relationship to the wider world. I have encountered groups of christians thrilled with their relationships with the body of Christ, yet with little obvious concern for their non-christian neighbours. Attention given to other pictures will help us to correct this. If we think of the church as 'proclaimer' we shall take seriously our responsibility to announce the gospel to the non-christian world (see 1 Peter 2.9; Matthew 28.19–20). The picture of the 'bride' of Christ (Ephesians 5.25–33) speaks of the church as the object of Christ's love. The 'vine' imagery of John 15 emphasizes the church's dependence on Christ for its life and strength. To picture the church as 'salt' and 'light' (Matthew 5.13–16) underlines our responsibility to display christian values in our involvement in the world. To think of ourselves as 'the people of God' (Romans 9.24–26; 1 Peter 2.9) reminds us of our relationship with the jews, who were called God's people.

Naturally, not all of these and other pictures can be at the front of our minds all the time. Different ones will seem more important to us in different circumstances. But there is a great variety to explore, and our doctrine of the church must allow room for them all.

The place of women

The third area to look at is one where the issue of 'cultural relativity' becomes prominent. How do we grapple with the teaching about the submissiveness of women in society and in the church? This is found in Paul (Ephesians 5.22; Colossians 3.18; and the instructions about women keeping silent in church, 1 Corinthians 14.34; and not being permitted to teach or have authority over men, 1 Timothy 2.8–15). It is also present in 1 Peter 3, which we shall look at more closely here.

Many christians believe that the instruction, 'You wives must submit to your husbands' (1 Peter 3.1) is a command for all times and all circumstances, a divinely ordered pattern for marriage. I want to suggest why the principles of interpretation described in this book lead to a different conclusion.

What is the *context* of Peter's message? He is writing from Rome to christians scattered around Turkey. In his day, the position of women was inferior to that of men, whether they lived in jewish, Greek or Roman society. Under jewish law a wife was owned by her husband and had no rights of her own. According to some jewish teachers, a man could divorce his wife for so trivial an offence as burning the toast. She had no right at all to divorce him. The pious jew offered thanks to God that he wasn't born a slave, a gentile or a woman. In the Greek and Roman worlds, too, women were mostly confined to the home, except for special events like weddings and funerals. If a woman went out a lot, she was suspected of being immoral. Most women received no education, and were not thought fit to join in conversation about politics and philosophy. But some women in Rome and elsewhere tried to break out of this subjection by getting involved in new religions which came in from the east. They dressed in low-cut dresses, got dolled up in elaborate hair-dos, and went in procession to secret worship sessions. And Roman society was scandalized by it all.

Add to this the fact that Peter's readers are facing persecution (1.8; 4.12) and that many of his women readers have non-christian husbands (3.1). Against that background, what should Peter write? Submit to your husbands, he says. You bear your christian witness by accepting your position and living in a Christ-like way, not by being provocative and overthrowing the conventions of society. And don't let your dress and hair-do raise suspicion that you're like those women attracted to secret eastern cults (verses 1–3). It would be crazy in the circumstances to suggest otherwise. Similarly today, if christians face persecution in a fanatically Moslem country, it would be suicide for the church's witness, if christian women paid no respect to Islamic convention.

But does this pattern of submissiveness apply to all places and at all times? To take the Bible seriously doesn't always mean taking it at face value. To understand the *significance* of Peter's message for us, we must notice how it differs from the conventional ideas of his time. Many people outside christian circles – jewish teachers, Greek and Roman philosophers – gave instruction about how women and slaves must submit to those in authority over them. Peter follows the pattern, but with three crucial differences.

First, he sets it all in the context of *mutual* submission. This whole section on submissiveness begins at 2.13, 'For the sake of the Lord submit to every human authority'. *All* christians are called to submit to each other, to give ourselves to each other in service. So there is a submission of husbands to wives, just as there is a submission of wives to husbands.

Secondly, Peter addresses wives directly. In the Greek and Roman literature on this topic, the writers normally don't address the women themselves. After all, women aren't educated, so can't be expected to understand these sorts of discussion. So the writers address the husbands, telling them how to organize their wives. But Peter speaks to the wives themselves, as people worthy of respect and able to judge for themselves the response which God invites from them.

Thirdly, there is instruction for the husband (verse 7), not about his authority over his wife, but about his respect and care for her.

And not only must we see how Peter's message is different from that of his non-christian contemporaries. We must take account of how our society differs from his. Women have the vote, education, and equal rights in law. For all these reasons we can't simply repeat literally the pattern of husband-wife relationships which Peter is working with. When we read the instructions to slaves in 1 Peter 2.18–25, we don't use it to argue that slavery should continue. We say that Peter's respect for slaves as people loved by Christ *had* to lead eventually to the emancipation of slaves. The whole structure of society based on slavery was being changed from within. And there is a similar logic to the teaching about wives. We are called not simply to repeat the pattern laid down in 1 Peter 3. That is relative to Peter's first-century culture. We are called to see how his message actually began to change the status of women, and then to ask how Christian values can make marriages better now.

There are guidelines for this in Peter's message of mutual submissiveness, his emphasis that the inner life is more important than outward show (verse 4), his exhortation to husbands to be sensitive and considerate (verse 7). A marriage is a place to demonstrate that to follow Jesus means to learn from him that greatness consists not in exercising power, but in self-giving service (Mark 10.42–45).

I don't expect every reader to agree with all I have said in this chapter. But I hope that the examples discussed will illustrate how a proper approach to the New Testament should stimulate our thinking about christian belief, and challenge some of our assumptions. If you disagree with conclusions to which I have pointed, you will need to show *in what ways* I have failed to use the New

Testament properly. When christians make constructive criticism of each other's views and explain *why* they disagree, there is hope of progress.

Thinking about doctrine involves an interplay between tradition, our situation, and scripture itself. Tradition is the filter which colours our view of biblical teaching. For instance, if in my church tradition, infants are baptized, I will be inclined to view biblical texts about baptism differently from someone from a baptist tradition. Our situation will often throw up questions which send us to the Bible in search of an answer, or will bring to life issues which previously have not concerned us. For instance, someone who lives in a community of several races and religions is faced with the question of how God views people of other faiths, and turns to the New Testament for guidance. Tradition and the situation will help to frame our questions and will influence our perspective, but they must not in the end dictate the answers. The New Testament itself must do that.

Summary

Our discussion of doctrine began with the insistence that doctrine must be built on the guidelines for interpretation explained in earlier chapters. These guidelines enable us to avoid such dangers as taking texts in isolation from their context. It was argued that development in doctrine is right and necessary, but development must be shown to be consistent with New Testament teaching. There was discussion of issues (the ascension; exorcism) which may create particular problems for people today if taken at face value.

Commitment to the authority of scripture requires us to look for unity as well as diversity in New Testament teaching, and to study the total witness of the New

Testament on a particular theme. We are also called to take seriously teaching which we find hard to accept, and to keep listening to scripture's own concerns rather than imposing our own concerns on it.

Three different issues in doctrine were then presented, the resurrection of Jesus, on which the New Testament speaks with a single clear voice; the church and its ministry, on which variety is as significant as unity; and the position of women, on which the issue of cultural relativity suggests different guidelines to us from some specific instructions given in the New Testament.

Questions for discussion

1 How can we resist the temptation always to read the New Testament with *our* questions, *our* preconceived ideas? (see page 113).

2 Do you think that the New Testament permits us to affirm belief in Jesus' resurrection without believing that his tomb was empty on the third day?

3 'New Testament teaching about the Church and its ministry shows remarkable variety, and our commitment to scripture requires us to take that variety seriously' (page 116). Do you agree? How does your answer affect your view of other church denominations and their ministers?

4 Do you think that this chapter's discussion of the place of women in society is a legitimate interpretation of the New Testament? Give reasons for agreeing or disagreeing with it.

8

The New Testament and christian spirituality

In this chapter and the next we come to the heart of what, for most christians, is the point of reading the Bible and learning about it. We want to grow in our relationship to Christ, and to get guidance from scripture about how to live as christians. These two aspects of christian living can't really be separated. Any spirituality which isn't coupled with christian obedience cannot be genuine christian spirituality. But, for convenience, we shall think about spirituality now, and behaviour or ethics in chapter nine.

A New Testament basis for spirituality

As we approach the Bible for guidance about the spiritual life, we can find in it a six-fold pattern on which a healthy relationship with God may be built. I suggest, first, that the New Testament comes to us as *invitation*. Before he announces anything else, Jesus announces the good news that God is at work to bring men and women close to himself: 'The right time has come, and the Kingdom of God is near!' (Mark 1.15). To people who have nothing to offer, no reason to be treated with special favours, he says, 'Happy are you poor; the Kingdom of God is yours!' (Luke 6.20). Parable after parable presses home the point that God's acceptance of us is a matter of his sheer grace, not of our deserving. It is the tax collector and not the pharisee who went home from the temple in the right with God (Luke 18.14). God is like the owner of the vineyard who pays generously even those workers who arrive only at the eleventh hour (Matthew 20.15). The invitation of Jesus is, 'Come to me, all of you who are tired from carrying heavy loads, and I will give you rest. Take my yoke and put it on you and learn from me . . .' (Matthew 11.28–29). The christian life begins with an invitation.

And it continues on the same basis. Paul, whose great word 'grace' expresses his discovery that salvation is God's *gift* to us through Christ, insists that the christian life depends on God's grace from start to finish. When the christians in Galatia are tempted to insist on the need to keep the Old Testament law, he reminds them that their spiritual life depends on God's *gift* of the Holy Spirit: 'How can you be so foolish! You began by God's Spirit; do you now want to finish by your own power? (Galatians 3.3). So the New Testament message is, first and foremost, an invitation to receive what God longs to give.

Secondly, the New Testament comes to us as *promise*. The whole Bible is full of the promises of a God who keeps faith with his people. David Livingstone, commenting on years of experience in Africa, quoted Jesus' final promise to be with his followers always, to the end of the age (Matthew 28.20), and added: 'Jesus Christ is a perfect gentleman, who never breaks his word'. This does not, of course, mean that we can take any promise of God in scripture and apply it to ourselves without regard to its context. Take, for example, Jesus' words in Matthew 10.19–20: 'Do not worry about what you are going to say or how you will say it; when the time comes, you will be given what you will say. For the words you will speak will not be yours; they will come from the Spirit of your Father speaking through you.' Preachers are sometimes tempted to rely on this promise as an excuse for not preparing their sermons. Lack of preparation, they suggest, will show their dependence on God's Spirit. But preachers ought to know better. For the context is the threat of persecution, and verse 19 actually begins, 'When they bring you to trial, do not worry about what you are going to say . . .' In *that* context, God's promise, to stand by those who suffer for Christ's sake, is secure. But we have no permission to apply it generally in all circumstances.

There are, however, many promises in scripture which are for all of us and which can form the basis of reflection and prayer. For instance, Jesus, in the context of general teaching about prayer, says, 'Bad as you are, you know how to give good things to your children. How much more, then, will the Father in heaven give the Holy Spirit to those who ask him!' (Luke 11.13). That promise is a secure starting-point for all of us who long to know more of God and his influence in our lives. We can confidently pray for what God has promised.

Christians have always used the promises of the Bible as a basis for prayer, as we can see from the many allusions to scripture in this extract from prayers used by christians in Rome around AD 95:

> Grant us, O Lord, we beseech you, your help and protection. Deliver the afflicted, pity the lowly, raise the fallen, reveal yourself to the needy, heal the sick, and bring home your wandering people. Feed the hungry, ransom the captive, support the weak, comfort the faint-hearted. Let all the nations of the earth know that you alone are God, that Jesus Christ is your Servant, and that we are your people and the sheep of your pasture' (1 Clement 59).

Through such regular use in liturgy, or through the practice of memorizing passages of scripture, the promises of God become part of our 'mind-set', ready to be drawn on at any time.

Thirdly, the New Testament comes as *demand*. We are called to turn from our sins and believe the Good News because the kingdom of God has drawn near (Mark 1.15). We are commanded to love God and our neighbour in response to God's love for us (Mark 12.28–34). The 'farewell discourse' in John 14–16 has much to say on the theme, 'If you love me, you will obey my commandments' (John 14.15). And the New Testament letters are full of exhortation to christian living. The classic example of this is Romans, where explanation of God's grace towards jew and gentile (chapters 1–11) is followed by exhortation to christian living in response to God's grace (chapters 12–15). There is no side-stepping the demand of God. But it is the demand not of a God determined to squeeze from us every ounce of obedience, but of a God whose own character, displayed in Christ, is to give himself for us all.

The fourth characteristic of the New Testament is that it is *Christ-centred*. 'Ignorance of the scriptures is ignorance of Christ', wrote St Jerome, who made the Latin Vulgate translation of the Bible. And knowledge of the scriptures brings knowledge of Christ, for the scriptures bear witness to him and show us how to live in relationship to him. So a key question about any New Testament passage which we study will be: What does it show me of Christ? What does it say about who he is, what he has done, what his purpose is for the church and the world, and what is involved in following him?

Fifthly, the New Testament is *a people's book*. It is addressed not primarily to individuals, but to churches and groups of christians; the gospels and letters were written for churches. Only 1 and 2 Timothy, Titus and Philemon are addressed to individuals. To remember this makes a difference to how we read passages such as the exhortations in Paul's letters. For instance, when we read the passage in Ephesians 6 about the armour which protects us against the attacks of evil, we are inclined to picture an individual soldier and see ourselves as standing alone against the enemy. But the passage is addressed to christians *together*. It is about our standing together against evil, like a whole cohort of Roman soldiers, united, disciplined and supporting each other. Or in Colossians 3.15, when Paul speaks of Christ's peace guiding us in decisions we make, he is talking not about decisions made individually and privately, but about decisions made together. That is how God's guidance generally comes, not through private flashes of enlightenment, but through discussion and prayer with others.

Finally, the New Testament comes to us as a message of *hope*. Ever since God called Abraham from Haran and promised him a new future in a new land (Genesis 12), God has been pointing his people towards the future. He sets before us that perfect kingdom to which he calls us. This means that the christian life is always forward-looking. We can't go back to our past, which is familiar to us and where security seems to lie. We are being called forward into new challenges, new possibilities for growth and development. This 'forward movement' also means that we don't have to be weighed down by our past failures and inadequacies. They are behind us, and in front of us is – God, and all the possibilities of life empowered by his Spirit. (See Philippians 3.12–14 for a vivid statement of this perspective.)

Biblical patterns of spirituality

I believe that the six points discussed above provide a secure framework for our thinking about christian spirituality. As we read the New Testament, we can ask whether the emphasis in a passage about christian living is an invitation or promise, demand or hope, or a combination of these themes. We can ask how it points to Christ, and how our application of it is affected by its being addressed to christians as a group.

Another way of exploring spirituality is to see what we can learn from the spiritual life of a particular person or writer. We could explore the gospels to discover the pattern of Jesus' praying. Mark 1.32–37, for instance, suggests a pattern, a rhythm of work and withdrawal from work, in which prayer is central (verse 35). If we study Luke's gospel especially, we see how Jesus is presented as praying at moments of crisis and decision (Luke 3.21; 6.12; 9.18, 28–29). We see that every recorded prayer of Jesus in the gospels, except his cry from the cross (Mark 15.34), begins with the word 'Father'.

Scholars agree that underlying this word in the Greek New Testament is the Aramaic word *Abba* which Jesus himself would have used, and which appears in its original language in Mark 14.36. It's an intimate family word – 'Daddy', 'dear Father' – which no one before Jesus had dared to use in direct address to God. But as well as intimacy with God, it also implies costly obedience to the Father's will. For it is in Gethsemane, where Jesus steels himself to carry out God's purpose, that the word appears on his lips. So when he invites his followers to address God in the same way, he is calling us not only to an intimacy with God, but also to total obedience. That he *does* so invite us is clear from Paul's use of *Abba* ('my father', *GNB*) in Romans 8.15 and Galatians 4.6. Such a study of Jesus' *practice* of prayer – in one particular gospel, or in all the gospels – will give stimulus and greater depth to our study of Jesus' *teaching* about prayer. This is found, for example, in Matthew 6.5–15; Luke 11.1–13; 18.1–14; John 14.9–14; 15.1–17.

Or we could study Paul's pattern of sprituality, seen at its most personal in 2 Corinthians. The key to it is the theme of 'God's strength in my weakness' which is expressed in 2 Corinthians 4.7–15 and 12.7–10. A different pattern, more suited perhaps to some personalities and some situations, is presented in Hebrews 11. Here the life of faith is pictured in terms of looking forward to the future which God has prepared, hanging on to him through the dark and puzzling periods, being confident that, despite all appearances to the contrary, his purpose will one day triumph.

Different passages, different approaches

As I argued in chapters two to five, different kinds of literature in the New Testament must be handled in rather different ways. Here are two or three examples of how this relates to spirituality.

We may study actual prayers in the New Testament, rather as we might study a Psalm in the Old. (Donald Coggan's book *The Prayers of the New Testament* (Hodder, 1967), is a classic which offers much help here.) Apart from prayers of Jesus there is, for example, a prayer of the early Church in Acts 4.24–30. And we overhear Paul praying in Ephesians 1.15–23; 3.14–21; Philippians 1.9–11; Colossians 1.9–14. We shall gain insight from such passages if we ask questions like these:

How does the prayer relate to the circumstances of the one who prays and the people prayed for?

What understanding of God's character and purpose does the prayer imply?

What specifically is requested in the prayer, and how does that compare with the things on which *our* prayers tend to be focused?

In thinking about this last question, I am struck by the focus in Colossians 1 on prayer for knowledge of God's will, for spiritual wisdom, and strength to do good and to endure suffering. It makes me ask whether those elements figure prominently enough in my prayer for others.

When we read *narrative* passages, a different approach is called for, requiring use of the imagination. One way of getting food for thought is to take a passage and try to 'get inside' the characters one by one. A group studying a passage together can share out the characters between them and, after individual thought, share what they have discovered about the character they have explored. For instance, in John's narrative of Jesus' arrest, trial and crucifixion (John 18–19) there are numerous characters who each 'represent' different attitudes to Jesus. In imagination we can 'get inside' each one in turn – Caiaphas, who was concerned to keep the peace; Peter, who denied Jesus; Pilate, who could find no fault with Jesus yet feared to be called 'not the Emperor's friend' (19.12). And so on. We can ask ourselves *why* they react in the way they do, and how much we find their reactions mirrored in our own fears and hopes, sins and prejudices. Such imaginative reflection will not become unhelpfully subjective as long as it is related to a careful reading of the text.

A variation on this is the way of meditating on a Bible passage taught by St Ignatius of Loyola. After reading the narrative two or three times, put down the Bible and become a character in the story. Use your senses to see, hear, smell and touch what is happening around you. As you picture yourself while the narrative unfolds, what is God saying to you in and through it? Let me illustrate this method in the words of a friend:

> I went on an Ignatian retreat feeling jaded with Bible reading. It wasn't that I had stopped reading it but it had lost its freshness. I was given an hour to read and reflect on Mark 2.1–12. It seemed to me a long time for twelve verses! However, I followed the

method deciding I would play the lead character! I pictured the crowd scene at Capernaum and what it looked like from the rooftop. Then I set about deciding which four people were to lower me through the roof. I could think of many I did *not* want but it was hard work deciding on four who would not drop me! As I dispensed with one after another I found myself thinking of all sorts of reasons why I would not trust this one or that one. I became uncomfortably aware that I had problems in trusting people. Independence may be a virtue but what happens when the chips are down and one needs support? So I too was paralysed though not with lifeless limbs. The name of my paralysis was mistrust. This felt painfully real and not at all like play-acting! As I lay on my stretcher before Jesus there was much to think about. Why was trusting so hard and why did I shrink from so many? What was there about the few that make me feel safe? And did I really want to be healed? As I spoke to Jesus and he to me the hour passed like ten minutes.

Afterwards, I wrote it all down in my journal and have often had cause to re-read it in the ongoing journey of healing God has for me.

I don't wish to suggest that this is the only way to study such a passage. Indeed, it may seem a little out of step with my argument in chapter two that we must look for the *main* point of the passage. But it is one way in which the message of a story can be explored. And my friend's account illustrates how, when one approach to Bible study seems repetitive and unproductive, a different approach can open up fresh channels for God's grace.

Apart from prayer passages and narratives, there are exhortations of many kinds in the New Testament. Many of these are deceptively straightforward, and may leave us unmoved by their very bluntness. Here the important thing often is to give our minds time to work out the implications of a biblical command or exhortation. I remember reading these words: 'Whoever says that he remains in union with God should live just as Jesus Christ did' (1 John 2.6). The uncompromising nature of this demand hit me between the eyes. The one thing I couldn't do was rush on to the next verse. I had to allow time for God to guide my thinking about how this 'imitation of Christ' might work out in my own life.

When scripture stops us in our tracks

This experience of being 'hit' by a passage of scripture is quite common. People speak of being stopped in their tracks, or they say that a flash of new light has come, revealing God to them. Certainly God does sometimes speak to us through scripture in a special personal way. But we must be careful at such moments not to abandon a responsible approach to understanding the New Testament. The Lord in his mercy does sometimes use a dubious interpretation of a misunderstood translation of the Bible to bring some message home to us. But that is no reason to expect him to speak normally in this way. It is no excuse for lazy Bible study which doesn't get to grips with what the biblical author meant to say. It's not enough to claim that such a method of getting 'blessed thoughts' or guidance from the Bible 'works'. You can get a nylon stocking to 'work' as an emergency fan-belt in your car, but that's no reason for advocating that all cars be fitted with nylons.

God has given us minds to think about the meaning of scripture. Notice how Paul, for all his emphasis on gifts of the Spirit, constantly appeals to reason and uses rational arguments to persuade his readers that a particular course of action is God's will (e.g., 1 Corinthians 6.12–20; 8.1–13). And God has given us other christians, with whom we can check our insights into scriptures. We have no right to use scripture as a peg on which to hang our personal spiritual fantasies.

To be more positive, there are undoubtedly many occasions when God 'hits' us by bringing home to us a very personal application of a passage. C.T. Studd, England cricketer in the 1880s and missionary pioneer in China, faced opposition from his family to his plans for missionary service. Agonizing over this conflict, he spent a sleepless night. 'But it seemed as though I heard someone say these words over and over, "Ask of Me and I will give thee the heathen for thine inheritance, and the uttermost parts of the earth for thy possession" (N. P. Grubb, *C.T. Studd, Cricketer and Pioneer* (1933) p. 40). That to him was the voice of God, which confirmed the rightness of going to China. It was not an obvious application of Psalm 2, line 8, but there is a certain logic about applying it in this way. Originally addressed to the king, the psalm came to be applied in Judaism to the expected Messiah who would be descended from King David. Hence, by a natural extension of meaning, what is promised to the Messiah is promised also to the Messiah's people. And so it came to C.T. Studd as confirmation of his role in the mission of Jesus the Messiah. And of course it was set in the context of months of thinking about the call to China. So different aspects of God's working in Studd's life and God's speaking to him were being blended together. It would be an utterly different matter if I opened my Bible at random, read 'I would like to see you on my way to Spain' (Romans 15.24), and concluded that the Lord was telling me to go to the Costa Brava for my holidays.

All God's speaking to us – whether in dramatic ways or through the steady absorption of the New Testament's message – is meant not to make us feel good but to transform us. For C.T. Studd it meant the abandoning of wealth and privilege, and a life of service in China, and later in India and Africa. His response to scripture that night influenced the lives of thousands.

Summary

This chapter has suggested that the New Testament offers a framework for christian spirituality. It comes to us as invitation, promise, demand; it is Christ-centred, is addressed to christians in community and is a message of hope. We can learn from biblical patterns of spirituality as we study, for example, how Jesus, Paul and the writer to the Hebrews speak of their relationship with God. We can learn about prayer by studying actual prayers in the New Testament, and by getting inside the characters of New Testament stories. We listen to exhortations in the New Testament by giving time to working out their implications for us and allowing God's Spirit to work on our hearts and minds.

The final section considers the moments when God seems to speak very dramatically or specifically through a passage which 'hits' us with startling force. We do well to be suspicious of interpretations which come at such times if they can't be defended according to proper principles of interpretation.

Questions for discussion

1 The chapter began by describing a 'six-fold pattern on which a healthy relationship with God may be built'. Would you add any other features of New Testament teaching which you feel are important for a healthy spirituality?

2 How may we 'claim the promises of God' for our spiritual benefit? How may we know when promises in the Bible are meant to apply to us?

3 Does the New Testament suggest guidelines which would prevent our spirituality from becoming a selfish pursuit of spiritual experiences?

4 Take one of the passages mentioned on page 130 and study it, using the questions and approaches suggested there.

9

The New Testament and christian behaviour

A friend of mine led a christian youth-group through a series of discussions on modern ethical issues such as nuclear warfare, abortion and sex ethics. When he asked them, 'Does the fact that you're a christian make any difference to your views?', each one answered 'No'. Like many others, they were living their lives in two separate compartments. Their christianity was concerned with spiritual and personal matters, but was largely irrelevant to the 'real world' of work, politics and the moral dilemmas of society.

Yet, if the Bible has no influence on our thinking about such ethical and social issues, we are admitting that the lordship of Christ doesn't touch us at many crucial points of our lives. So how far can we look to the Bible for instruction about behaviour? There are, of course, a number of dificulties which must be acknowledged before we look for answers.

Problems in using the Bible for guidance in ethics

The first problem is that scripture doesn't actually say anything about many of the issues which concern us. It knows nothing of genetic engineering, star-wars or multinational corporations. So how can we work out a christian view on such matters? Rummaging through the Bible for texts which might just have some bearing on such issues seems about as appropriate as using the workshop manual for a philistine chariot to service a Ford Sierra.

Secondly, there is the problem of cultural relativity, already discussed in chapter six. The Bible's instructions were originally given in a world which generally took for granted attitudes towards slavery, monarchy, family life and many other issues. How can we apply them in our very different world? Are they simply irrelevant now? After all, not many of us take much notice of Jesus' command that his followers wash each other's feet (John 13.14).

A third difficulty is that different instructions are given in different parts of the Bible. Not only are there differences between the Old and New Testaments, for example, in attitudes to war, or rules about what meat may be eaten. Within the New Testament, too, there are differences. In Mark 10.11, for example, Jesus apparently forbids divorce for any reason, whereas in Matthew 19.9 divorce on the grounds of unfaithfulness is permitted.

Fourthly, there is the question whether biblical instruction to christians can be applied to society in general. If, for example, I believe as a christian that sexual relations outside marriage are wrong, can I, and should I, urge that this principle be incorporated into the laws of my country?

Finally, there is sometimes the sheer difficulty of knowing how to apply a biblical command in our situation. What does it mean for me to carry a soldier's pack two kilometres? If someone asks me for something, should I always give it to him? (Matthew 5.41–42).

Before trying to solve some of these problems in our study of New Testament teaching, let me make two other introductory points. First, it should not worry us to discover that much of the New Testament's ethical teaching is not unique to christianity. We saw in chapter seven how Peter's letter takes over from the jewish, Greek and Roman world familiar patterns of teaching about the state, slavery and family life – though he adds to it a distinctive 'twist' which he shares with other New Testament writers. And much of Jesus' teaching isn't new. A few decades earlier a gentile challenged the great jewish teacher, Hillel, 'Make me a proselyte (a convert) on condition that you teach me the whole law while I stand on one foot.' Hillel replied, 'What you hate for yourself, do not do to your neighbour: this is the whole law, the rest is commentary. Go and learn.' This is echoed in Mark 12.28–34 and especially in Matthew 7.12. But notice that Jesus' saying is positive – 'Do for others what you want them to do for you'. The point I am making is that it shouldn't surprise us to find that much of the New Testament's ethical teaching is not distinctive. Insight into what kinds of behaviour make for a healthy society is not confined to christians. Of course not, and we should rejoice that christian ideals are often shared by others.

The other point is that the Bible is not our only source of guidance for making ethical decisions. If we ask, for instance, in what circumstances it may be right to fight a war, there is a long tradition of discussion on this issue that would help us to make up our minds. And with modern warfare, particularly, there is a lot of technical information without which an informed decision can't be made. What would be the likely effect of a nuclear bomb dropped on Birmingham or Leningrad or Chicago? What difference in practice is there between nuclear weapons classified as offensive and those classified as defensive? And so on. Answers to such questions, as well as to questions about the Bible, will influence our verdict. This book is about the New Testament, but we must not imagine the New Testament will tell us the whole story.

Commands in the New Testament

As we turn to the Bible itself, we think first about the ethical commands to be found there. We shall concentrate on examples in the teaching of Jesus. We know that Jesus' words can't always be taken literally as though he were giving detailed rules for every circumstance of life. For his complaint against the pharisees was precisely that their zeal for applying the Old Testament law in minute detail made them blind to 'the really important teachings of the Law, such as justice and mercy and honesty' (Matthew 23.23). There is something dreadfully wrong if someone needs a rule-book to tell him how to act when he comes across a man mugged on the way to Jericho.

Yet to say that Jesus' commands are not a set of rules doesn't permit us to sidestep their force. Only those who hear Jesus' words and *obey* them are like the wise builder whose house stands secure against the storms of judgement day (Matthew 7.24–27). So what does it mean to obey his words?

It is helpful to distinguish three different kinds of commands in Jesus' teaching. First, there is the genuine commandment. There is only one example of this – 'Love the Lord your God . . . and love your neighbour as you love yourself' (Mark 12.30–31). This infinitely demanding command to love the neighbour is central to Jesus' teaching about behaviour. He extended the traditional understanding of 'neighbour' so as to include *all* people, even the samaritan (Luke 10.25–37) and the enemy (Luke 6.27–36). He made clear that love means *caring action*. The good samaritan loved his neighbour, not because he felt for him, but because he actively 'was kind to him' (Luke 10.37). Jesus made clear that the demands of love go far beyond the rules laid down by any law. The priest and the levite broke no law, but only the good samaritan showed love.

The second kind of command – of which there are many – are in fact illustrations of how the basic command to love works out in specific situations. This can be seen in Luke 6.27–31, where the basic command to 'love your enemies' is followed by instances of what this means. For example, when someone curses you, to love means to respond with blessing (verse 28). Then comes the saying which summarizes the nature of love – doing for others what you want them to do for you. This may not sound very profound, but it is a down-to-earth practical test which would transform relationships in an instant if it were taken seriously. How often would we utter harsh words about someone, or take someone for granted, if this saying of Jesus were written in our hearts?

To apply such illustrative sayings with unimaginative literalism is to destroy their real purpose. 'If anyone hits you on one cheek, let him hit the other one too' (Luke 6.29). Originally, this verse referred to an insulting blow from someone who attacks the christian for his allegiance to Christ. Jesus instructs this disciple not to take his attacker to court, but to accept more attacks, if necessary, in a spirit of love. In our culture this precise situation is unlikely to arise. Yet we can see it as a practical example of Jesus' call to respond to hurts and insults not by retaliation ('an eye for an eye') but by positive love. He wants to replace a natural human reaction with a better way. And it isn't hard to imagine ourselves in situations where a similar demand is made of us. Jesus' demand may raise a doubt in our minds: if we respond to insults in the way he insists, won't that encourage people to think we're 'soft', too feeble to stand up for ourselves? Taken on its own, the saying might suggest that. But if we take Jesus' teaching about love *as a whole*, and especially his own *practice* of love, we can see that genuine love is tough. Whereas 'an eye for an eye' simply maintains the present situation, love transforms both people and situations.

The third kind of command consists of urgent exhortations. For instance, 'Be concerned above everything else with the Kingdom of God and with what he requires of you . . .' (Matthew 6.33). Or Jesus' word to the rich man: 'Go and sell all you have and give the money to the poor . . .' (Mark 10.21). As we saw in chapter three, this is not a universal rule, but a drastic remedy for this particular man's problem. But, of course, for others who share his problem of being too tied to their wealth, the same remedy may be required.

Often these exhortations are expressed in a deliberately exaggerated way in order to underline the point. 'If your hand makes you lose your faith, cut it off!' (Mark 9.43). *Any* measure is worth taking to avoid losing one's place in God's kingdom.

A sample passage: Luke 6.20–49

It may help to illustrate what we've seen so far, by looking through a section of teaching in Luke (his equivalent to the Sermon on the Mount in Matthew 5–7). This is not a detailed study, but simply a few notes on Jesus' ethical teaching here.

He begins with the contrasting beatitudes – 'Happy are you . . .' – and woes – 'How terrible for you . . .' (verses 20–26). This group of sayings serves both as gospel and as warning. It is gospel because it promises God's kingdom and its blessings to those who are needy. In Jesus' message the good news that a new life is offered by God comes *before* the demand of a new lifestyle. It is a warning because it warns of the consequences of ignoring God's invitation to the kingdom. Hence the passage shows by implication what attitudes are required of the would-be disciple.

There follows in verses 27–36 the teaching about love for enemies to which we have referred already. The basic command to love without restriction is illustrated by specific examples in verses 27–31. Verses 29–30 illustrate the generosity of spirit which is a thousand miles away from the calculating 'justice-at-all-costs' attitude which is so familiar in human relations. But isn't Jesus going a bit far when he says, 'Give to everyone who asks (begs) you for something, and when someone takes (steals) what is yours, do not ask for it back' (Verse 30)? Perhaps this is one of those exaggerated sayings, delivered with a wry smile. Because it is not a rule to be taken literally, it doesn't demand that I always give money to a tramp even though I'm sure he'll spend it on methylated spirits. It doesn't mean I must meekly hand over my garden tools to my neighbour even though he never gets round to bringing them back. Yet what I cannot do is sidestep the force of these sayings by simply doing nothing when confronted by the tramp or the neighbour. To love means to abandon a calculating meanness and to risk being generous in the face of need.

Verses 32–36 explain *why* such an attitude is demanded. 'Tit-for-tat' love is nothing to be proud of – any human being can manage that! The love which Jesus expects of his followers is nothing less than a reflection of God's love, 'for he is good to the ungrateful and the wicked' (verse 35). In showing that kind of love they show themselves to be genuine sons of God. The calling of christians, and their 'reward' (verse 35), is to reflect God's character.

Further examples of loving action are given in the teaching about judging others (verses 37–42). The opening command – 'Do not judge others, and God will not judge you' – is probably equivalent in meaning to the second – 'Do not condemn others, and God will not condemn you'. It does not mean that it's wrong for a judge to pass sentence in court, or for an examiner to pass or fail his students. Jesus is referring to the judgemental, 'holier-than-thou' attitude often adopted by religious people.

Verses 39–40 make the proverbial point that a disciple becomes like his teacher. If, then, he learns from Christ, he will not be like the pharisees, blind leaders of the blind. To learn from Christ involves not being critical of others (verse 37), but being self-critical (verses 41–42). The saying about the speck and the log shows Jesus making a serious point with a touch of humour. Why are we so reluctant to realize that Jesus could be funny?

The final two paragraphs express two basic principles of Jesus' ethical teaching. The image of the tree and its fruit (verses 43–45) shows how actions spring from a person's inner character. Hence Jesus' constant concern about attitudes and motives rather than simply with outward deeds, and his insistence that people need to be changed from within. Lastly, the picture of the two builders (verses 46–49) declares that obedience to Jesus' words is an absolute demand for the disciple. Only those who listen to his words and obey them will 'stand' on the day of judgement. And this underlines the fact that Jesus' ethical teaching is not merely wise advice about how to make society better. It is a description of the response which God calls for. And the nature of our response – or lack of it – affects our eternal destiny.

So the sermon in Luke 6 takes us into some of the most important and persistent features of Jesus' teaching. It shows us how ethics is based on, and is a response to, the gospel. It shows us Jesus' concern with inner character rather than merely with outward action. It includes the basic command to love followed by several instances of what that means in particular situations. But it doesn't present grave problems of application, because the instances given are near enough to situations which we ourselves encounter.

Finding principles

Often, however, we have to work harder at drawing *principles* from New Testament commands, in order to apply them today. In chapter four we saw how this might be done with Paul's passage about meat sacrificed to idols (1 Corinthians 8–10). The important thing is to ask not merely *what* the biblical writer says, but *why* he says it. This enables us to get behind the text – which may be dealing with a situation quite remote from us – to the motives, the principles, the understanding of God which underlie the text. Take Paul's words in Philippians 4.2: 'Euodia and Syntyche, please, I beg you, try to agree as sisters in the Lord.' (Imagine how they felt when attention was suddenly focused on them as Paul's letter was read out to the assembled church in Philippi!) Clearly underlying this exhortation is the principle that settling squabbles is part of what love among christian brothers and sisters requires. And we can apply that in all kinds of situations without knowing any more about Euodia and Syntyche.

Instructions about slaves and masters, as in Ephesians 6.5–9, are more tricky. We can't apply them straightforwardly to modern work-situations because workers are not slaves, they are not owned by their employers. And the nature of work in a complex industrial world is vastly different from what it was for the slaves whom Paul addressed. Yet there are principles here which will give us a starting-point for thinking about work and about relationships between employer and employee. Paul shows how the gospel transforms all human relationships, including those between master and slave. The power of the master is limited through the recognition that he is responsible to a Master in heaven. The slave's work is given value and dignity when he sees it as being offered to God and not merely to his master. The master too – 'in the same way' (verse 9) – is to offer his treatment of his slaves as his service to the Lord. Here are some of the raw materials for industrial relations. A christian would want to argue for relationships and structures in industry which affirm that people matter as people, not merely as cogs in a machine. He would argue that employers and managers have obligations to their employees, as well as employees having obligations. And he would urge that there should be limits to the power of employers, and protection for employees from loss of human dignity. But these are *only* raw materials. *How* these principles may be applied in a particular work-situation depends on many technical and practical factors. The important issue here is that a christian can never be content to let working practice be determined solely by non-human factors such as efficiency or profit.

Ethics by example

We have looked so far at *commands* in the New Testament, which point us to particular kinds of behaviour. But we may also find guidance from stories in the Bible which offer examples to follow – or avoid. I know someone in the building trade who found courage to refuse a shady deal which was proposed to him because the previous evening his Bible study group had studied how Joseph had maintained his integrity against the advances of Potiphar's wife (Genesis 39).

The difficulty with looking for examples to follow is that biblical stories don't always make it clear whether the incident related is something which meets with God's approval or not. For instance, when Paul stood before the Council of elders in Jerusalem, he addressed the high priest Ananias, 'God will certainly strike you – you white-washed wall!' When told that he had just insulted the high priest, Paul answered, 'I did not know that he was the high priest'. And then he provoked a division of opinion between pharisees and sadducees on the Council (see Acts 23.1–11). Now was Paul really unaware that he was addressing the high priest? Or was he being sarcastic, or deceptive? Was it a legitimate tactic to stir up argument between pharisees and sadducees so as to divert attention from himself? The passage leaves us guessing about all this, perhaps because Luke's main purpose is to show how Paul was preserved by God in the face of jewish hostility, so that he could bear witness in Rome (see verse 11).

In other places, however, a narrative *does* show a particular action meets with God's approval or disapproval, and we can learn from that. In the story of Ananias (not the high priest, nor the Ananias who helped Paul in Acts 9!) and Sapphira, God's disapproval of their action is clear from the way in which their sudden deaths are interpreted as divine judgement (Acts 5). So there is a solemn lesson in their story which Luke intends us to learn. But notice that their sin was not that they withheld their property while everyone was selling his and giving the proceeds to the poor. It seems clear from Acts 4.32–37 that the selling of property was a voluntary action, and that those who sold didn't necessarily sell everything they possessed. The sin of Ananias and Sapphira was the *deception* whereby they pretended to give the proceeds of the sale whilst keeping part of it for themselves. Any application of the story should focus on this issue of deception.

Another story which offers an example from which much can be learnt, is in John 13. Here Jesus washes the diciples' feet, and then demands that the example be followed: 'I, your Lord and Teacher, have just washed your feet. You, then, should wash one another's feet' (verse 14). We have no choice about this example story because

Jesus gives a command to go with it. Yet few of us ever wash each other's feet, because foot-washing is 'culture-relative' to a culture where sandals are worn, roads are hot and dust is plentiful. But the whole presentation of the story in John offers us a powerful picture of our Lord giving himself in humble service, and calling his followers to do the same. What form humble service will take will vary enormously from one situation to another, but there is no sidestepping this demand to follow in the footsteps of the Servant of all.

Ethics from doctrinal themes

There is another way of getting at principles for behaviour. It is more oblique, but is especially important for ethical questions on which the Bible gives no explicit instruction. It involves starting from basic christian beliefs and working out their implications for ethics.

The starting-point is our belief about *creation*. From this, several conclusions which are important for ethics can be drawn. God is Lord over his whole creation. He has made mankind to live responsibly towards him and towards each other. He has made male and female to complement each other. He has commissioned the human race as 'stewards' over the world, accountable to him for our use of the earth's resources. He expects people to engage in productive work, according to a pattern of work and rest symbolized by the presence of the sabbath among the days of the week. All this is expressed in the early chapters of Genesis and affirmed in the rest of scripture.

The doctrine of the *fall*-man's disobedience against God as portrayed in Genesis 3 – tells us that evil has worked its way into every aspect of God's creation. Not only is mankind's relationship to God affected. Relationships among people became fragile and disrupted. Hence the Bible recognizes that ethics can't be taught as an ideal system of behaviour for an ideal world. It has to allow for human weakness and social evil. So, for example, it will insist on legal controls to limit the exploitation of one person or group by another.

But we also affirm belief in *redemption*. God has not abandoned the world to sin and self-destruction, but has entered into his creation in the person of Jesus, to deliver and transform it. So there is the opportunity of forgiveness and of a new pattern of life demonstrated by Christ and empowered by his Spirit.

A final theme we may mention is the hope of *the kingdom of God*. Christian ethics has a basic optimism because of this conviction that the day will come when God completes the work of redemption. Then the biblical promise of a kingdom which is just, peaceful, universal and permanent will be fulfilled. And this hope is not mere 'pie in the sky' because Jesus in his ministry has already shown the power of God's kingdom at work. The vision of how the world will ultimately be sets before us goals to aim for, values to work by, in all our concerns to change society for the better. If, for instance, God's ultimate purpose is that human relationships should be characterized by justice and peace, then justice and peace are primary goals in christian ethics because they express what God wants.

I have already dropped hints as to how themes such as these may influence our approach to questions about personal behaviour and goals for society. But let's take them a little further with examples from three areas of concern. On the day I write, a report has appeared about how young Blacks in Hackney, in the east end of London, feel about their place in British society. Most of them feel that they are not accepted as belonging here. They feel discriminated against when looking for work. Many of those in school, though born in Britain, speak a mixture of Creole and standard English. Hence 79% of them say they often have difficulty understanding what their teachers are talking about. A christian approach to this problem would draw on our four themes. The creation theme affirms that all people are equally valued by God and therefore discrimination, where it exists, must be resisted. The fall theme recognizes that prejudice, weakness, laziness and the bleakness of many people's social environment contribute to the problem and must be faced realistically. The redemption theme reminds us that God is concerned especially with the powerless and the neglected, and offers the possibility of a new beginning. The kingdom theme urges us to believe that things don't always have to remain as they are, and points to justice and peace as goals to aim at. 'Peace', by the way, doesn't mean in the Bible simply absence of hostility, but harmony and good relations within oneself, with God, and with others.

Set out like that, our approach can sound quite glib. These themes are only a beginning, and must be related to detailed information about the situation and realism about other factors such as the level of available resources. But the approach to any such issue must have *reasons* for proposing a particular policy, and it is from such themes that christian reasons and policies are to be worked out.

Marriage and divorce

A second difficult area is the question of divorce. Many christians assume that appeal to a particular text (Mark 10.11–12) will settle the issue by banning divorce completely. Other texts may modify the position a little. Divorce is permitted on grounds of unfaithfulness (Matthew 19.9; the *GNB* translation is peculiar here), or when a non-christian partner insists on it (1 Corinthians 7.15). But while these texts are to be taken with utter seriousness, they cannot on their own decide the issue for us. As I have often insisted in this book, there are questions to ask about the *context* of Jesus' teaching. How, if at all, do we allow for the fact that Jesus was speaking in a context where Moses' permission of divorce (Deuteronomy 24.1–4) was being abused by men out of selfish lack of concern for their wives? But we must also bear in mind our doctrinal themes. Jesus himself appealed to the creation theme when he asserted, quoting Genesis 2.24, that a man unites with his wife and 'the two will become one'. That is God's ideal, so that divorce is always in some sense bad, an admission of failure. But in our view of marriage and divorce must there not be some place for recognizing human weakness and sinfulness? If we mean what we say about forgiveness and the possibility of a new beginning, what will that imply? If, for example, a couple marry too young, before they understand themselves or each other, and learn gradually that they are really quite unsuited to each other, does a christian view of marriage require that they be 'imprisoned' with each other for the rest of their lives?

World development

Lastly, there is the issue of world development which, along with the nuclear question, will be *the* great moral issue for the foreseeable future. Here again we are surrounded by a vast array of complex economic and technical questions which must be part of any detailed treatment of the problem. But our themes can provide a framework of guidelines to help us respond to these questions about poverty and the imbalance between nations of the rich north and the poor south.

The creation theme tells us that human beings are stewards of the created world and are meant to control it through work. The fact that all people are created by God implies that we are all of equal value to him, and have a responsibility to care about each other's welfare. The tea planter in Sri Lanka has no less right to a reasonable standard of living than I have. And we saw earlier that a distinctive feature of Jesus' ethic is its universal character. Caring for each other's welfare is not something that can stop at the boundary of 'my community' or 'my nation'. In principle it extends worldwide. Within this context of mutual responsibility, there is a particular obligation for the rich to care for the poor and needy. This is a matter not only of compassion or charity, but of justice. It is little use sending my five pounds for famine relief in Africa if the whole political policy of my country is designed to maintain an international monetary and trade system which effectively denies to poor nations fair access to world markets.

Work, though part of man's calling, isn't possible without access to resources – land, energy, education, for example. The key problem in many poor countries is that most people are denied access to land, and therefore can't produce anything. That is a problem of injustice within the country, and one possible course of action would be to encourage christians within the country to work for social change.

Realism about human sinfulness enables us not to be surprised that vested interests and desire to hold on to power make it very hard for rich nations, or for rich people within poor nations, to transfer resources to poorer nations. This is why it was sensible for the Brandt Report, *North–South: A Programme for Survival* (Pan, 1980), to argue that its proposals for reform of trade and monetary systems were to the advantage of rich as well as of poor nations. Such an appeal to self-interest might succeed where to use only high-sounding moral arguments would fall on deaf ears.

The redemption theme reminds us again of God's concern for the outcast and oppressed. And the hope of the kingdom, with its vision of the future, suggests that we should be less bothered with how the world came to be in its present crisis – 'Who's responsible for this injustice?' – than with solutions for getting out of it – 'What response should we make?'

Once again, I stress that we are dealing with a vastly complex issue for which the Bible has no tidy answers. But it does give guidelines which deserve to be heard. We need more, not less genuinely moral input in this debate, if it is not to rumble on at the level of short-term, political self-interest.

Are biblical ethics only for believers?

The whole idea of relating biblical themes to such global issues may make us uneasy. Aren't the moral teachings of Old and New Testaments meant only for jews and christians? Have we any right to impose them on anyone else? The short answer – and there is no space for a longer one – goes something like this. We advocate biblical ethical principles for society at large because biblical ethics express the way human beings and human relationships are designed to work best. Any society, whether composed entirely of christians or entirely of atheists, can only work satisfactorily if people normally speak the truth, refrain from stealing and killing, and so on. Even the rascally landlord who exploits his tenants in low-standard housing relies for his success on *other* people keeping the rules. He knows that tenants will pay the rent, that his bank manager will keep his money safe and that most citizens will not try to steal his Rolls-Royce or run off with his wife.

So our reason for advocating biblical moral standards for society is, that as christians, we believe that they express God's will for his creatures. God doesn't have one will for christians and something entirely different for others. Our argument for biblical standards, when faced by people who do not share our beliefs, will be that in practice society works better when such standards are generally accepted.

Nevertheless, the New Testament does, of course, make demands on christians which go deeper than anything which can be imposed on others or enshrined in a legal code. Jesus' contrasts in Matthew 5.21–48 illustrate this clearly. For instance, 'You have heard that people were told in the past, "Do not commit murder . . ." But now I tell you, whoever is angry with his brother will be brought to trial . . .' (Matthew 5.21–22). Constantly he presses us to go further along the way to behaviour which reflects the character of God himself.

There are many difficulties in working out christian ethics, and this chapter has been making illustrative suggestions rather than an ethical system. But in the end, the greatest challenge is illustrated by a comment which once came my way when I was an 'A' level examiner. The exam paper asked candidates to 'comment on points of difficulty' in Romans 13.8: 'Be under obligation to no one – the only obligation you have is to love one another. Whoever does this has obeyed the Law.' And a girl from Uganda began, 'The difficulty here is that it is not always easy to love your neighbour. It is obvious that one cannot love everyone as one loves oneself, and this is the difficulty.' It certainly is!

This is where we need to hear not only the demand but the promise of the Holy Spirit's power for christian action. Constantly in Paul's letters, for example, the demand and the promise are interwoven. The demand that we should not be proud or irritate one another in

Galatians 5.26 is preceded by the assurance that the Spirit produces love, joy, peace . . . (verse 22–23). And the two are linked by verse 25: 'The Spirit has given us life; he must also control our lives'.

The Bible isn't a cook-book with a detailed recipe for every modern situation. But the Bible's message is what makes christians the people they are – people of love and insight and judgement, able to think responsibly about God's will for the present. The Bible makes the christian, and the christian responds to situations in a christian way.

Summary

Our discussion of the Bible and christian behaviour first mentioned some of the problems of getting guidance from scripture. We then studied ways of drawing ethical guidance from different kinds of material in the New Testament. First, there are commands, which we divided into three types: the basic command to love, commands which are actually illustrations of the love-command in specific situations, and urgent exhortations to follow Christ's way. Luke 6.20–49 was used as a sample text to illustrate essential features of Jesus' ethical teaching. The next section discussed how principles can be drawn from New Testament commands and applied to modern situations.

After the discussion of commands, the use of stories for moral instruction was examined. Then we saw how the doctrinal themes of creation, the fall, redemption and the hope of the kingdom of God can provide guidelines for ethics. This is especially so for issues where specific biblical guidance is minimal or non-existent.

Finally we asked whether biblical ethics can be applied to a secular society.

Questions for discussion

1 Is the attitude mentioned in the first paragraph of this chapter a common one, in your experience? How can we help people to be more deeply *christian* in their approach to questions of behaviour?

2 It has been suggested that the New Testament's ethical teaching 'acts as a compass rather than as an ordnance survey map', since it is meant to set our lives in the right direction rather than to give detailed rules for specific situations. Do you agree?

3 'Not many of us take much notice of Jesus' command that his followers wash each other's feet (John 13.14)' (page 138). Why not? If this passage is not to be taken at face value, what *does* it teach about christian behaviour in your group?

4 Take an ethical issue which has recently been in the news, and try to form a christian judgement on it. Does the Bible give specific teaching which can be applied to the situation? What bearing do the themes of creation, the fall, redemption and the kingdom of God have on the question? What factors apart from biblical teaching need to be considered?

10

Approaching group bible-study

Nearly all the books of the Bible were written for communities of believers. Not until developments in printing methods made books comparatively cheap was it common for people to read the Bible on their own. Before that, and still today in many cultures, the Bible's message has been learnt and studied by groups of christians meeting together. And in recent years, many christians in western countries have been rediscovering the particular benefits and challenges of studying in groups. This brief chapter will draw together what has been explored in the rest of the book and make some practical suggestions about group study.

The story so far

The key to effective understanding of the Bible is to ask the right questions. Our exploration in this book has pinpointed the following questions as being perhaps the most important questions to ask of a book or passage.

1 What kind of a book is it?

How is our understanding of it influenced by the fact that it is a gospel, a letter, or Acts or Revelation?

2 What is the form of the passage?

How is our understanding of it influenced by the fact that it is (for example) a miracle story or a parable, a piece of exhortation or a prayer?

3 What did the passage mean for its writer and original readers?

3.1 What is the context of the passage?

3.1.1 What is its historical, geographical, religious and cultural context, and how will that influence our understanding of it?
3.1.2 What is its context in the book to which it belongs? How is our understanding affected by the fact that it comes at *this* point in the book, *after* what has gone before and *before* what comes next?

3.2 What is the content of the passage?
3.2.1 What do the words mean?
3.2.2 What do the sentences mean?
3.2.3 What do the paragraphs mean?

4 What is the significance of the passage for us?
4.1 What principles does the passage express?
Truths about God and his purpose?
Truths about ourselves?
Guidelines for spirituality and behaviour?

4.2 How do they apply to us?
4.2.1 How does the problem of cultural relativity affect our application of the passage?
4.2.2 Apart from the general significance of the passage for today, what specific response or action does it call for from us as individuals or as a group?

Set out like that, the questions look lifeless and uninviting. But they are valuable as a check-list to ensure that we are studying the Bible responsibly. And questions which look dull on paper have a habit of transforming people's lives when they are actually *asked*. Suppose we wrote down a set of 'questions to ask when considering getting engaged', and the first question was, 'Will you marry me?' It would look pretty dull and predictable on paper, but not when put by one individual to another! When Philip met the Ethiopian eunuch as he studied Isaiah 53, the Ethiopian asked a simple enough question: 'Of whom is the prophet saying this? Of himself or of someone else?' (Acts 8.34). But it was the right question to ask, and led to his discovery of Jesus as the suffering servant whose death meant the offer of life to all people.

Before thinking a little more about methods of Bible study, let's look at the attitude with which we should approach it.

Attitudes to Bible study

The first requirement is that we come to the Bible with an attitude of *listening to God*. Our main purpose is not to air opinions, nor to learn about Israelite worship, but to open our hearts and minds to God. We expect to be taught, guided, nourished by him through our study. And that will not happen without a proper reverence – not a reverence for print on paper, but for God who addresses us through the Bible. How different from the ancient rabbi of whom it was said, 'When Rabbi Eliezer expounds, he begins by saying, "Scripture, be silent, while I am interpreting"!'

Because we are listening for God to address us, we will approach the text honestly. We will not insult God by lifting texts out of context, nor by getting 'blessed thoughts' from a passage without grappling seriously with what the author meant to say. And we shall recognize the importance of studying a wide range of biblical material, not just our favourite bits of John or Romans or Psalms. For God has more to say to us than can be said through the favourite bits we've discovered so far!

Secondly, we pray for *the Holy Spirit's guidance*. Because the scriptures were inspired by God's Spirit (2 Timothy 3.16; 2 Peter 1.20–21) God's Spirit will enlighten our understanding and application of them. John's gospel especially draws attention to his work of revealing the truth about God (John 14.17; 15.26; 16.13), teaching and pointing people to Christ (14.26; 15.26; 16.14).

Thirdly, we *listen to others*. One of the exciting things about studying scripture in a group is that we learn from other people's insights. Because of who they are and the experiences they've been through, they notice things in the Bible which have never occurred to us. So they become a channel through whom God speaks to us from scripture. Another benefit is that we can test out our own understanding with people we trust. Sometimes people go wrong in their faith simply because through constant study on their own they get pet theories and strange ideas which are never submitted to comment from other christians.

Within a group there will be some who are more experienced and knowledgeable about the Bible than others. They can, of course, be a pain in the neck if they insist on parading their knowledge and telling us all about the meaning of the Greek. But if they have the humility which is required of any Bible student, they are an asset. We shouldn't despise knowledge of the Greek text or of the New Testament's first-century background, just because it's unlikely that everyone in the group has such knowledge. A proper understanding of the variety of gifts in the Church will enable us to rejoice in the gifts of those with greater knowledge than ourselves and to use them as resources for the group. Equally, the group member who as yet has little knowledge is not to be despised. The person who brings only questions and no answers can be a key person for the success of the group's learning.

Fourthly, Bible study is of no value unless it *leads to action*. The truth of God does not come to people who sit in pious circles debating the finer points. 'The Bible is food for wrestlers', D.T. Niles used to say. It is in wrestling with what is to happen *after* the Bible has been studied that we discover scripture speaking to us with the authentic voice of God. 'Whoever is willing to do what

God wants,' said Jesus, 'will know whether what I teach comes from God or whether I speak on my own authority' (John 7.17).

Methods of study

What is the ideal size for a study group? I would say between six and ten people. If there are fewer than six, there may not be enough variety of contributions. If there are more than ten, not everyone will feel able to contribute.

It's important for any group to have realistic goals to aim at. And for most groups this means that a series of six or eight studies on one book or theme is as much as they can cope with. Not many groups will relish a twenty-two week series on the book of Revelation or a twenty-eight week series on Matthew's gospel. Far better to spend, say, five weeks on the Sermon on the Mount (Matthew 5–7), and then move on to something different. Perhaps a study of a short New Testament letter, or selected passages from Romans. Or, instead of working through a book or series of chapters, take a doctrinal theme or an ethical issue and study what is taught in several parts of the Bible.

Let's imagine we've decided to study the first letter of John, a chapter at a time, and the first study is in chapter 1. The leader's task is not to lecture, but to enable the group to dig out from the passage what John said to his readers and what God is saying to us. A few words of introduction will be needed, but not much more is necessary than what is said in the *Good News Bible*, p. 297. It will highlight for us the fact that the letter's main concern is with what christians believe about Christ, and how we are to maintain fellowship with each other in the face of destructive false teaching. It will be worth pointing out to the group that all the sentences in the letter which begin 'If we say . . .', or 'Whoever says . . .', or 'Anyone who denies . . .' seems to be allusions to what the false teachers were teaching. (See 1.8, 10; 2.4, 9; 2.23; 4.20.) If we explore those statements in the course of our five-week study, we shall be doing justice to the *context* of the letter which calls forth the response of John.

The study proceeds by the leader asking questions to provoke searching of the passage and discussion of people's findings. The leader will have studied the passage beforehand to grasp the main issues for himself, and to decide on appropriate questions. He (or she) will probably have used a commentary or study-guide, so that he can give guidance if people raise questions about puzzling verses. But he will refrain from telling them everything he has learnt unless they get stuck.

Questions must be designed to help the group discover the *content* of the passage, and then to explore its significance for us. They must not be too complicated ('In view of the Johannine Logos theology, how do you understand the soteriological purport of verse 1?'). They must not be insultingly obvious ('What is the message we have heard, according to verse 5?'). They should normally be such as to make people think about the *meaning* of a verse or word, rather than simply repeating what it says. They shouldn't be phrased in such a way as to presuppose the answer which the leader wants ('Don't you think we should confess our sins daily to God, in view of verse 9?'). One question which should *never* be asked is, 'Has anyone got any thoughts about the passage?' It is aimless, and encourages people to produce ideas which are only vaguely related to the text.

So what questions might be appropriate for 1 John chapter 1? We should divide the passage into two sections, and frame questions such as these.

Verses 1–4

1 If John's readers were being disturbed by false teaching, why did he think it important to begin with this statement of eye-witness testimony to Jesus?

2 What is it about Jesus that John wishes to convey by calling him 'the Word of life, which has existed from the very beginning' (verse 1)?

3 Why do you think John's writing would make his joy complete?

4 What does the passage say which you think is particularly important for our belief about Christ?

5 How important is it for christians to be in agreement about our beliefs, in order to have fellowship with each other and with God (verse 3)?

Verses 5–10

6 What do you think it means to say that 'God is light' (verse 5)?

7 Verse 6 speaks of the danger that there may be a 'credibility gap' between what we claim to believe and how we behave. In what ways do you think *we* are inclined to say one thing, and practise another? (Encourage *honest* discussion.)

8 How can we 'live in the light' (verse 7)? (Notice the connection between our being in the light and God being in the light.)

9 Why do you think John stresses the importance of confessing sins (verse 9)? Is there a danger that constant confession makes us 'comfortable' with our sins rather than leading us away from them?

10 In what ways will our study of this passage take us a

step forward in our belief about Christ, our relationship to God, and our relationship to each other? (If members of the group are fairly at ease with each other, the leader may invite each in turn to express one thing he has learnt and will take away with him.)

Of these ten questions, numbers 1, 2, 3, 6 are concerned mainly with *content*, numbers 4, 5, 7, 8, 10 mainly with the passage's significance for us. Number 9 links content and significance.

Of course, questions need adapting for different groups. The ones suggested here might be too difficult, or too easy, or may need refocusing in the light of the group's needs. And it may be felt that my questions do not point strongly enough towards action aroused by the study. I think that is fair comment, but we can't force issues into a passage if they aren't there already. The rest of the letter will point to plenty of practical actions which the group may need to take.

When the study is over, the leader should evaluate how it has gone. Did the questions prove too difficult? Did I enable people to get to grips with the passage? Was I too tolerant of people going off into irrelevant discussion? Did the discussion suggest that people were making discoveries about the truth of God and his will for us? Only if we ask such questions and are prepared to be self-critical shall we improve our competence as leaders. It will help to ask one or two of the group members how they found it – sometimes a leader can be blissfully unaware that he talked too much, or squashed a tentative contribution, or allowed the discussion to focus on secondary issues rather than the main points of a passage.

Other methods of study

The method of study described above is followed by many groups. But there is a whole host of variations which are worth trying if they would suit the group and the topic to be studied.

For instance, people can be asked to study a passage beforehand, with some questions to get them going. Or a meeting can begin with time for people to think on their own or in a small group about the passage. Or, if you are studying a topic for which several different passages are relevant, different groups can concentrate on different passages and then share their findings. Approaches like this are useful if the numbers are too large for one group.

Role play can help people to get inside the characters of a narrative. Members of the group who volunteer or are chosen to act the characters are given a few minutes to prepare their roles, and then act it out. Other members will sympathize with the actors' role in the story, so that as soon as the drama is finished the leader can ask 'How did you feel about . . .?' 'What did you learn about Jesus, or about your own character in the story . . .?' See further the discussion of getting inside a narrative in chapter eight (pages 131–2).

The so-called Swedish method of Bible study (so-called because it was first used by young christians in Sweden in the 1940s) is especially useful for passages in the letters and for parables. But it can often be used with narratives too. Give each person a piece of paper with the following symbols down the left-hand side:

Ask them to study the passage and write down what they learn under each of the five headings: an arrow pointing up – something about God; an arrow pointing down – something about human nature; a candle – a new insight; a question mark – something not clearly understood; a horizontal arrow – a command to obey.

After a few minutes invite people to share what they have written, and develop discussion from that. Try it with 1 John 1!

Sometimes a group will want to start from a question or a topic rather than a passage. People may want to learn about the Holy Spirit, or apartheid, or Sunday trading, or bringing up a family. Such issues may involve looking at various parts of scripture and handling awkward questions about how to apply them to modern situations. So it is probably best either to ask a suitable person to introduce the study with a short talk, or to use one of the many sets of study materials which are available. See the suggestions about resources below.

Finally, let it always be remembered what we are studying the Bible for. When I watch a Shakespeare play, it may be helpful to have read books about it, studied different interpretations of its meaning, heard the actors talk about how it feels to play Hamlet, or Lady Macbeth. But in the end all those helps must be put quietly to one side so that the play itself can address me and I can become involved with its message. And if that is true of a play, how much more is it true of the Bible. We must learn all we can about helpful ways to study it and interpret it correctly. But then we must sit with the Bible itself, and allow it to bring us face to face with God and his will.

Resources for Further Study

For many people, a vast array of 'Bible study aids can be daunting and unhelpful. They can keep us away from the Bible rather than lead us into it. But access to certain resource materials will help anyone studying the Bible to discover its riches and to deal with tricky questions that crop up. In particular, those who lead study groups will gain confidence from having a few resources on hand during their preparation.

These are the kinds of things to consider. I m not suggesting you get all the items listed, but you may decide that one or two of them are just what you need. I mention mostly types of material rather than specific books, since some books so quickly go out of print. See what your nearest Christian bookshop currently has available! But I include a few books which are likely to have a reasonably long life.

1. **A Bible dictionary.** Among other things, this will give an outline of the contents of all biblical books. It will tell you about people and places, and will explain important themes in the Bible. There are cheap pocket-sized dictionaries such as *The Hearthside Bible Dictionary* (Cumberland House, Nashville USA), published in UK as the Macmillan Dictionary of the Bible (Macmillan, London); and the *Bible Dictionary* in Nelson s Pocket Reference series (Thomas Nelson, Nashville USA). A larger one is the *New Bible Dictionary* (IVP, Downer s Grove USA/Leicester UK).

2. **A survey of the content and themes of each biblical book.** This is invaluable if you are about to begin a series of studies of a particular book. It will introduce the book to you and give a short running commentary on it. My favourites are *The Bible Guide* by Andrew Knowles (Augsburg, Minneapolis USA; Lion, Oxford UK) and the slightly more detailed *Zondervan Handbook to the Bible* (Zondervan, Grand Rapids USA), published in UK as the *New Lion*

Handbook to the Bible (Lion, Oxford). If you want a larger commentary on the whole Bible in one volume I suggest the *Oxford Bible Commentary* (Oxford University Press, New York/Oxford) or the New Bible Commentary (IVP, Downers Grove USA/Leicester UK). There are also several good series of commentaries on individual biblical books (or groups of shorter books) designed for preachers and those seeking to apply the message to Christian living.

3. **A study Bible.** These are Bibles which as well as the biblical text include short introductions to each book and footnotes commenting on points of interest or difficulty. The danger of them is that readers may attach the same importance to the notes (which are sometimes merely the opinion of the writer) as to the biblical text itself. But sensibly used they can be a very handy guide. Look for books with 'Study Bible in the title. The notes will tend to reflect a particular doctrinal perspective on the Bible. For example, the *NIV Study Bible* (Zondervan, Grand Rapids USA/Hodder, London UK) is evangelical, while the *Oxford Study Bible* (Oxford University Press, New York USA/Oxford UK) represents the perspective of 'critical scholarship . A particular type of study Bible is the NIV Thematic Study Bible (Hodder, London UK), published also as the *NIV Thematic Reference Bible* (Zondervan, Grand Rapids, USA). As well as the biblical text, this includes a thematic section covering 2,000 topics, enabling the reader to draw together biblical material on a chosen topic. A boon to anyone wanting to find out what different parts of the Bible have to say about everything from Aaron to Zion, but including also themes such as time, materialism, sexuality, stress, etc.

4. **Books which discuss in more detail the questions of interpretation surveyed in this book**—and include the Old Testament as well as the New—especially Gordon Fee and Douglas Stuart, *How to Read the Bible for All Its Worth* (Zondervan, Grand Rapids, USA; Scripture Union, Milton Keynes UK).

5. **Booklets designed to guide group Bible study.** Typically, these provide an introduction to the nature and contents of the biblical book to be studied, and suggest discussion questions and group activities designed to enable understanding and application of the message. Here are series of such booklets to look out for: The Lifebuilder series (IVP, Downers Grove USA/Scripture Union, Milton Keynes UK) includes booklets both on specific biblical books and on topics of contemporary interest (pointing you to relevant biblical material to help you explore the topic), for example:
   • *20/30: Bible Study for Young Adults* (Abingdon, Nashville)
   • *Bodybuilders* (Scripture Union, Milton Keynes UK)

6. **Internet resources.** These can be a valuable source of freely available quality resources. But they need to be used with discernment because there is no one out there to guarantee the quality, and some of them represent narrowly defined doctrinal perspectives which you may not find helpful. So it is wise to follow the recommendation of someone you trust rather than just look up ‘Bible on a search engine. Here are two which I recommend:

   <www.bibegateway.org> gives you access to the text of the whole Bible in several translations, the facility to do find passages through word searches, and reliable commentaries on some biblical books.

   <www.damaris.org> offers imaginative study materials (some free, some at a fee) particularly aimed at providing a biblical perspective on issues of current concern and contemporary books and films. These are great for teenagers and young adults keen to think through what the Bible might have to say about issues in contemporary culture.

7. Finally, there are publishers specializing in producing **booklets of notes for those who wish to study the Bible daily** (or at least regularly!). Typically each booklet

provides notes for one or three months at a time, guiding you through biblical books sequentially (or selected passages linked by a theme), offering explanatory comments and suggestions for reflection, prayer and action. There are different 'levels' of notes to suit different age groups and stages of Christian maturity. Scripture Union provides such materials worldwide. In the UK the Bible Reading Fellowship is another excellent provider. The notes can be bought in a Christian bookshop or ordered regularly through your church. (If there is no agent for such notes in your church, maybe that's a role you could take up!)

Lightning Source UK Ltd.
Milton Keynes UK
15 December 2010

164396UK00001B/8/A

9 781894 667340